Math Fun Grade I

Best Value Books™

Table of Contents

ISBN 0-88724-439-4

About the book...

This book is just one in our Best Value™ series of reproducible, skill oriented activity books. Each book is developmentally appropriate and contains over 100 pages packed with educationally sound classroom-tested activities. Each book also contains free skill cards and resource pages filled with extended activity ideas.

The activities in this book have been developed to help students master the basic skills necessary to succeed in mathematics. The activities have been sequenced to help insure successful completion of the assigned tasks, thus building positive self-esteem as well as the self-confidence students need to meet academic and social challenges.

The activities may be used by themselves, as supplemental activities, or as enrichment material for the mathematics program.

Developed by teachers and tested by students, we never lost sight of the fact that if students don't stay motivated and involved, they will never truly grasp the skills being taught on a cognitive level.

About the authors...

Patricia Pedigo has many years of teaching experience in urban, rural, public, and private settings. She has taught at all elementary and middle school grade levels, and as a reading specialist. Patricia has created many of the materials that she uses in her classroom, using a blend of content area topics with language development methods. She holds an M.Ed. in Reading Education and is nearing completion of her doctoral studies.

Dr. Roger DeSanti has been an educator since the mid 1970's. His teaching experiences have spanned a wide range of grade and ability levels from deaf nursery school through university graduate school. As a professor, he has authored numerous articles, books, achievement tests, and instructional materials.

Senior Editors: Patricia Pedigo and Roger De Santi
Production Director: Homer Desrochers
Production: Arlene Evitts and Debra Ollier

Ready-To-Use Ideas and Activities

The activities in this book will help children master the basic skills necessary to become competent learners. Remember, as you read through the activities listed below and as you go through this book, that all children learn at their own rate. Although repetition is important, it is critical that we never lose sight of the fact that it is equally important to build children's self-esteem and self-confidence if we want them to become successful learners.

Flashcard ideas

The back of this book has removable flash cards that will be great for basic skill and enrichment activities. Pull the flash cards out and cut them apart (if you have access to a paper cutter, use that). Following are several ideas for use of the flash cards.

- Use the flash cards to practice and reinforce addition and subtraction facts.

- Have a child read the number sentences as they are held up. Allow them to "keep" the card if they correctly answer it within a specified time limit.

- Divide the flash cards into fact groups (tens, under eight, addition, etc.). Have the students work in small groups and practice giving the facts.

- Give each child three or four flash cards. Call out numbers and have students identify the number sentences in their pile that equal the called out number.

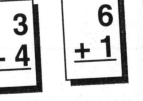

- Turn the flash cards with the number sentence showing. Have students match equivalent number sentences. Self-check by looking at the answers on the back of the card.

- Have students classify the flash cards according to their fact family. Groups of two, three or four may play "Go Fish" by asking players for equivalent number sentences.

Ready-To-Use Ideas and Activities

Play team "War". Divide the cards into two piles. Two students turn over the top two cards and answer the number sentence. The player with the highest answer takes both cards. Pass the pile on to the next student and repeat. The team with the most cards at the end wins.

Get a spinner and anything that will act as a three minute timer (a timer, stop watch, or watch with a second hand), or decide upon a certain number of rounds of play. In turn, each player spins the spinner twice and adds the two numbers together. The person with the most correct answers after a specific period of time or rounds wins. For example, one game will consist of six rounds of play. Whoever has the most points after six rounds of play wins. Each correct answer is worth one point.

As players memorize facts and gain confidence add another spin. When using more than two spins, the player should state the problem out loud and answer as they go. If for instance the spinner shows 1, 2, and 5, the player would say 1 plus 2 is "3" and 5 is "8".

For subtraction practice again use a spinner and always subtract the smaller number from the larger number. As confidence is gained add another spin. Players must always add the two or three largest numbers together and subtract the last one. When using more than two spins, the player should state the problem out loud and answer as they go. If there are four spins and the numbers are 3, 7, 5, and 3, the player in turn would say 7 plus 5 is "12", plus 3 is "15", minus 3 is "12".

Reproduce the bingo sheet included in this book, making enough to have one for each student. Hand them out to the students. Take the flash cards and write the problems on the chalk board. Have the students choose 24 of the problems and write them in any order on the empty spaces of their bingo cards, writing only one problem in each space.

Ready-To-Use Ideas and Activities

When all students have finished filling out their bingo cards, take the flash cards and make them in to a deck. Call out the answers one at a time. Any student who has a problem that equals the called out answer should make an "X" through the problem to cross it out. The student who crosses out five problems in a row first (horizontally, vertically, or diagonally) wins the game and shouts "BINGO!". Another fun version of this game is to write answers on the board and call out the problems. To extend the game you can continue playing until you a student crosses out all of the problems on his bingo sheet.

Challenge your own score! The next two pages include basic addition and subtraction problems which children should memorize. To help them we suggest you make multiple copies of these pages. Work on only one page at a time. Get a minute timer. See how many problems the child can do correctly in one minute. Record the child's score on a piece of paper. Let the child try again and see how many problems he/she can do correctly. The more times a child does each page, the higher his/her score will become and the more problems he/she will learn. As scores increase so does a child's self-confidence.

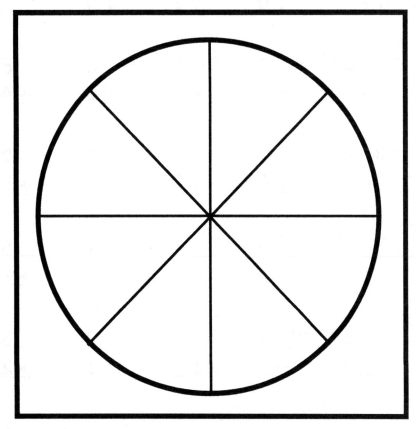

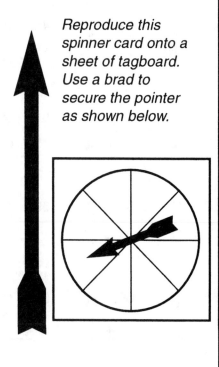

Reproduce this spinner card onto a sheet of tagboard. Use a brad to secure the pointer as shown below.

Name _____   Date_____

1. 1 +1	2. 3 +9	3. 4 +1	4. 7 +2	5. 1 +3	6. 4 +2	7. 7 +3	8. 4 +5
9. 6 +8	10. 2 +0	11. 1 +2	12. 1 +7	13. 8 +4	14. 7 +5	15. 2 +3	16. 4 +4
17. 7 +1	18. 1 +8	19. 2 +2	20. 4 +3	21. 2 +6	22. 6 +7	23. 1 +4	24. 7 +4
25. 6 +9	26. 1 +6	27. 7 +6	28. 9 +0	29. 2 +1	30. 1 +5	31. 6 +6	32. 3 +8
33. 5 +6	34. 1 +0	35. 2 +8	36. 3 +4	37. 4 +0	38. 1 +9	39. 6 +4	40. 7 +7
41. 6 +1	42. 2 +5	43. 7 +8	44. 5 +5	45. 2 +4	46. 3 +6	47. 5 +0	48. 5 +4
49. 3 +3	50. 4 +8	51. 7 +9	52. 4 +9	53. 5 +8	54. 5 +3	55. 6 +5	56. 2 +7
57. 5 +2	58. 5 +7	59. 2 +9	60. 9 +1	61. 6 +3	62. 4 +7	63. 7 +0	64. 5 +9
65. 6 +2	66. 5 +1	67. 3 +7	68. 8 +3	69. 4 +6	70. 6 +3	71. 8 +1	72. 8 +2

CD-3721

Hundreds Chart

1	2	3	4	5	6	7	8	9	10
11	12	13	14	15	16	17	18	19	20
21	22	23	24	25	26	27	28	29	30
31	32	33	34	35	36	37	38	39	40
41	42	43	44	45	46	47	48	49	50
51	52	53	54	55	56	57	58	59	60
61	62	63	64	65	66	67	68	69	70
71	72	73	74	75	76	77	78	79	80
81	82	83	84	85	86	87	88	89	90
91	92	93	94	95	96	97	98	99	100

Addition and Subtraction Table

+／−	0	1	2	3	4	5	6	7	8	9
0	0	1	2	3	4	5	6	7	8	9
1	1	2	3	4	5	6	7	8	9	10
2	2	3	4	5	6	7	8	9	10	11
3	3	4	5	6	7	8	9	10	11	12
4	4	5	6	7	8	9	10	11	12	13
5	5	6	7	8	9	10	11	12	13	14
6	6	7	8	9	10	11	12	13	14	15
7	7	8	9	10	11	12	13	14	15	16
8	8	9	10	11	12	13	14	15	16	17
9	9	10	11	12	13	14	15	16	17	18

 CD-3721

Hopscotch

Use your math facts to complete the hopscotch board.

1. 2 + 2 =   + 0 =   + 1 =

2. 1 + 1 =   + 0 =   + 2 =

3. 4 + 1 =   + 1 =   + 0 =

4. 3 + 1 =   + 1 =   + 1 =

5. 2 + 2 =   + 0 =   + 2 =

6. 0 + 0 =   + 2 =   + 3 =

Cross Challenge

Draw a line from a math expression in Column A to the number it equals in Column B. The first problem is done for you. In the boxes under Column C, draw the correct number of balls for each number.

Column A   Column B   Column C

4 + 2 ○

0 + 2 ○   ○ 0

3 + 3 ○
                      ○ 1
2 + 1 ○

5 + 1 ○   ○ 2

4 + 0 ○
                      ○ 3
3 + 1 ○

1 + 4 ○   ○ 4

2 + 3 ○
                      ○ 5
2 + 1 ○

1 + 1 ○   ○ 6

1 + 0 ○

Mystery Math

Look at the mystery number. Circle all math expressions in that row which equal the mystery number. The first problem is done for you.

Mystery Number	Math Expression			
0	1 + 3	(0 + 0)	1 + 0	0 + 2
6	1 + 5	1 + 4	3 + 3	4 + 2
1	6 + 0	2 + 3	1 + 0	1 + 1
3	2 + 2	3 + 0	2 + 1	4 + 1
5	2 + 1	4 + 1	3 + 2	1 + 3
2	2 + 1	2 + 0	5 + 1	1 + 1
4	1 + 3	2 + 2	1 + 4	5 + 1

Circle all the math expressions that equal 6.				
0 + 0	1 + 4	6 + 0	2 + 2	3 + 1
0 + 4	5 + 1	2 + 1	3 + 2	0 + 1
2 + 4	0 + 3	5 + 0	3 + 3	0 + 6

Leapfrog

Use your math facts to move across the lily pads.

1. 3 + 1 = ⬭ + 2 = ⬭

2. 2 + 0 = ⬭ + 4 = ⬭

3. 4 + 1 = ⬭ + 1 = ⬭

4. 2 + 3 = ⬭ + 1 = ⬭

5. 4 + 0 = ⬭ + 1 = ⬭

6. 1 + 1 = ⬭ + 2 = ⬭

7. 1 + 2 = ⬭ + 3 = ⬭

8. 3 + 3 = ⬭ + 0 = ⬭

9. 1 + 3 = ⬭ + 1 = ⬭

10. 2 + 2 = ⬭ + 2 = ⬭

Bonus

$$3 + 2$$

$$+ 0$$

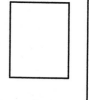

$$+ 1$$

CD-3721

Fact Finder

Solve each math sentence in the Facts Box. Search the puzzle for facts.
Circle the whole math sentence when you find it.

FACTS BOX

$0 + 2 =$ ___ $5 + 1 =$ ___ $3 + 3 =$ ___

$3 + 2 =$ ___ $2 + 4 =$ ___ $2 + 2 =$ ___

$0 + 3 =$ ___ $3 + 1 =$ ___ $1 + 4 =$ ___

$0 + 6 =$ ___

3	+	2	=	5	7	+	3
+	2	+	4	=	6	4	+
0	+	0	+	3	=	3	8
=	4	=	1	+	2	+	2
2	=	1	=	7	+	3	+
=	5	+	3	=	5	=	2
2	=	4	+	0	+	6	=
+	11	=	3	+	1	=	4
0	=	5	=	12	=	4	9
10	7	+	6	=	6	+	0

Bonus: Did you find a false math fact in the puzzle? Draw a red box around it.

Compare Sums

Compare the number sentences. Circle the expression that is larger. If they are equal, circle them both. The first problem is done for you.

1. 3 + 1   and   (4 + 2)

11. 6 + 0   and   2 + 3

2. 0 + 3   and   1 + 4

12. 0 + 4   and   2 + 2

3. 6 + 0   and   4 + 2

13. 0 + 5   and   4 + 1

4. 3 + 3   and   1 + 5

14. 0 + 2   and   1 + 4

5. 2 + 1   and   0 + 4

15. 1 + 5   and   2 + 3

6. 2 + 4   and   3 + 2

16. 4 + 2   and   0 + 5

7. 1 + 1   and   2 + 1

17. 2 + 3   and   0 + 5

8. 3 + 2   and   0 + 5

18. 4 + 1   and   3 + 1

9. 1 + 5   and   4 + 1

19. 3 + 2   and   1 + 5

10. 2 + 3   and   4 + 0

20. 3 + 1   and   0 + 3

Mystery Math

Look at the mystery number. Circle all math expressions in that row which equal the mystery number. The first problem is done for you.

Mystery Number	Math Expression			
0	6 - 0	(5 - 5)	(4 - 4)	(2 - 2)
4	5 - 1	3 - 2	3 - 3	6 - 2
1	6 - 5	1 - 0	2 - 1	3 - 2
3	4 - 1	3 - 0	4 - 2	3 - 0
5	3 - 1	6 - 1	3 - 2	5 - 0
2	2 - 0	4 - 3	3 - 1	2 - 1
4	6 - 2	5 - 1	3 - 0	4 - 0

Circle all the math expressions that equal 6.

5 - 1	4 - 3	6 - 3	2 - 2	5 - 1
6 - 4	5 - 1	2 - 2	4 - 1	6 - 6
3 - 3	3 - 3	6 - 0	4 - 3	2 - 1

Compare Differences

Compare the number sentences. Circle the expression that is larger. If they are equal, circle them both. The first problem is done for you.

1. 3 - 2   and   (4 - 1)

2. 3 - 3   and   1 - 0

3. 6 - 0   and   4 - 2

4. 3 - 1   and   1 - 1

5. 5 - 3   and   6 - 4

6. 4 - 4   and   3 - 2

7. 5 - 1   and   6 - 2

8. 3 - 2   and   6 - 5

9. 5 - 4   and   4 - 1

10. 2 - 1   and   4 - 0

11. 6 - 0   and   5 - 3

12. 5 - 4   and   2 - 2

13. 6 - 3   and   4 - 1

14. 0 - 0   and   4 - 4

15. 5 - 1   and   3 - 3

16. 4 - 2   and   6 - 4

17. 5 - 3   and   6 - 5

18. 4 - 2   and   3 - 1

19. 3 - 2   and   6 - 5

20. 3 - 1   and   6 - 3

Hopscotch

Use your math facts to complete the hopscotch board.

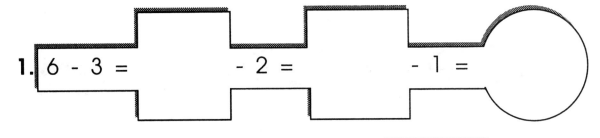

1. 6 - 3 =   - 2 =   - 1 =

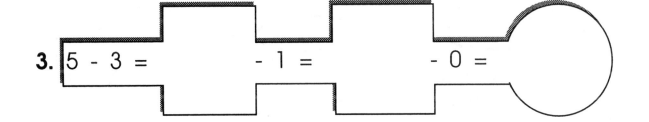

2. 4 - 2 =   - 1 =   - 1 =

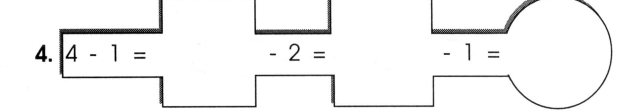

3. 5 - 3 =   - 1 =   - 0 =

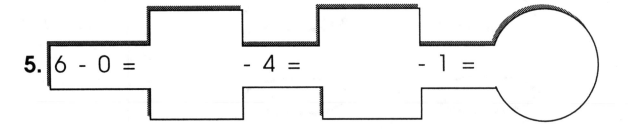

4. 4 - 1 =   - 2 =   - 1 =

5. 6 - 0 =   - 4 =   - 1 =

6. 5 - 1 =   - 2 =   - 0 =

Leapfrog
Use your math facts to move across the lily pads.

1. 3 - 1 = - 1 =

2. 5 - 3 = - 0 =

3. 4 - 2 = - 2 =

4. 6 - 3 = - 1 =

5. 4 - 0 = - 3 =

6. 5 - 1 = - 3 =

7. 3 - 0 = - 2 =

8. 4 - 3 = - 1 =

9. 6 - 1 = - 3 =

10. 6 - 2 = - 2 =

Bonus

$$6 - 2$$
$$- 1$$
$$- 2$$

Blankety- Blanks

Solve the problems below and write the answer in the box. On the blanket, shade in all the numbers that are in the answer boxes.
The answers will make a pattern.

$3 - 3 = \boxed{}$

$4 - \boxed{} = 1$

$6 - 5 = \boxed{}$

$\boxed{} - 4 = 2$

$5 - \boxed{} = 3$

$\boxed{} - 4 = 1$

$6 - \boxed{} = 2$

1	3
6	0
9	5
7	2
8	4

Name_____   Skill: Subtraction Facts to 6

Fact Finder

Solve each math sentence in the Facts Box. Search the puzzle for facts.
Circle the whole math sentence when you find it.

FACTS BOX

4 - 3 = ___   3 - 2 = ___   6 - 4 = ___

5 - 2 = ___   4 - 4 = ___   5 - 3 = ___

3 - 1 = ___   6 - 3 = ___   6 - 6 = ___

5 - 1 = ___

```
6  -  6  =  0  8  11  =
10 11  -  4  =  1  -   5
5  -  2  =  4  -  6   -
4  5  =  3  -  7  =   3
-  -  10 -  4  =  6   =
3  3  -  2  =  1  -   2
=  =  3  =  3  -  6   -
1  2  =  1  -  3  -   5
```

Bonus: Did you find a false math fact in the puzzle? Draw a red box around it.

©1996 Kelley Wingate Publications   14   CD-3721

Magic Trail

Follow the trail by solving math problems and find the magic number.

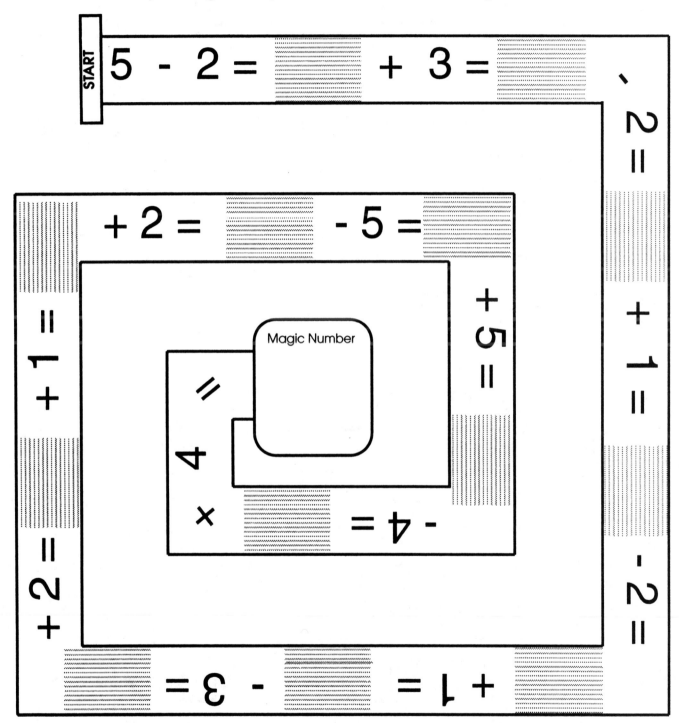

START 5 - 2 = [____] + 3 = [____]

` - 2 =

+ 1 =

- 2 =

+ 5 =

+ 2 = [____] - 5 = [____]

+ 1 =

+ 2 =

Magic Number

= 4 ×

- 4 =

+ 3 = [____] - [____] = 1 + [____]

MAGIC NUMBER _____

Hopscotch

Use your math facts to complete the hopscotch board.

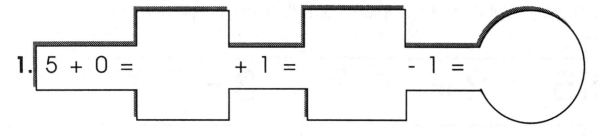

1. 5 + 0 =   + 1 =   - 1 =

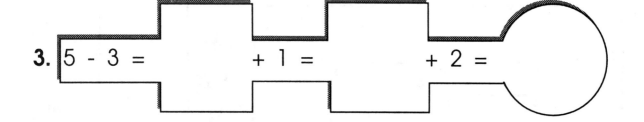

2. 4 - 2 =   + 2 =   + 1 =

3. 5 - 3 =   + 1 =   + 2 =

4. 3 - 3 =   + 3 =   + 3 =

5. 1 + 4 =   - 4 =   + 1 =

6. 3 + 1 =   - 4 =   + 6 =

Name_____

Hopscotch

Use your math facts to complete the hopscotch board.

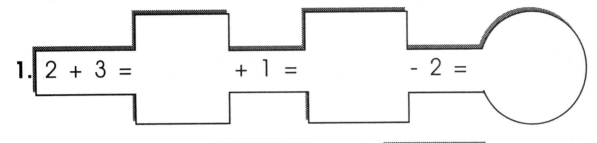

1. 2 + 3 =   + 1 =   - 2 =

2. 6 - 3 =   - 1 =   - 1 =

3. 4 - 3 =   + 2 =   - 1 =

4. 3 - 3 =   + 3 =   - 2 =

5. 6 - 4 =   - 1 =   + 2 =

6. 3 - 1 =   + 4 =   + 0 =

Mystery Math

Look at the mystery number. Circle all math expressions in that row which equal the mystery number. The first problem is done for you.

Mystery Number	Math Expression			
0	6 - 2	(4 - 4)	3 - 1	0 + 1
6	1 + 5	3 - 2	3 + 3	4 - 2
1	6 + 0	6 - 5	5 - 4	3 - 1
3	1 + 2	3 - 0	2 + 2	4 - 3
5	3 + 1	6 - 2	3 + 2	1 + 4
2	2 + 2	3 - 3	5 - 3	4 - 2
4	1 + 5	5 - 1	3 + 1	5 - 2

Circle all the math expressions that equal 5.

0 + 0	1 + 4	6 + 0	2 + 2	6 - 1
4 - 4	5 + 1	2 - 1	3 + 2	0 + 1
2 + 4	6 - 3	5 + 0	3 + 3	0 + 6

Leapfrog

Use your math facts to move across the lily pads.

1. 3 + 3 = ⬭ - 2 = ⬭

2. 6 - 3 = ⬭ + 2 = ⬭

3. 6 - 4 = ⬭ - 2 = ⬭

4. 1 + 3 = ⬭ - 2 = ⬭

5. 6 - 5 = ⬭ + 4 = ⬭

6. 2 + 4 = ⬭ - 3 = ⬭

7. 5 - 4 = ⬭ + 2 = ⬭

8. 5 + 0 = ⬭ - 1 = ⬭

9. 6 - 6 = ⬭ + 3 = ⬭

10. 5 - 2 = ⬭ + 1 = ⬭

Bonus

$$4 + 2$$

☐

$$- 5$$

☐

$$+ 3$$

☐

Compare Equations

Compare the number sentences. Circle the expression that is larger. If they are equal, circle them both. The first problem is done for you.

1. 3 - 1   and   (4 + 2)

2. 6 - 3   and   0 + 4

3. 5 + 0   and   4 - 2

4. 3 - 3   and   1 + 5

5. 3 + 1   and   0 + 4

6. 2 + 4   and   3 - 2

7. 5 - 1   and   2 + 1

8. 3 - 2   and   0 + 2

9. 1 + 5   and   4 + 2

10. 5 - 3   and   4 - 0

11. 3 + 0   and   2 + 1

12. 0 + 4   and   6 - 4

13. 6 - 5   and   4 - 1

14. 0 + 2   and   5 - 4

15. 1 + 4   and   6 - 3

16. 2 + 2   and   5 - 5

17. 4 - 3   and   0 + 2

18. 4 - 1   and   3 + 1

19. ͡ + 2   and   5 - 5

20. 3 - 1   and   0 + 3

Name_____

Family Facts Fiesta

Complete the families of math facts.

$\square + 5 = 6$

$1 + 5 = \square$

$6 - \square = 1$

$\square - 5 = 1$

$3 + \square = 5$

$\square + 2 = 5$

$3 + 2 = \square$

$\square - 2 = 3$

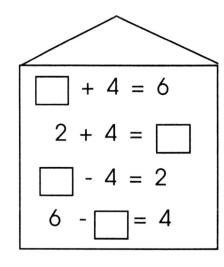

$\square + 4 = 6$

$2 + 4 = \square$

$\square - 4 = 2$

$6 - \square = 4$

$\square + 1 = 2$

$1 + \square = 2$

$2 - \square = 1$

$\square - 1 = 1$

$2 + \square = 3$

$1 + 2 = \square$

$3 - \square = 1$

$\square - 1 = 2$

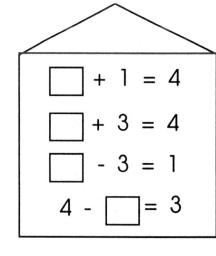

$\square + 1 = 4$

$\square + 3 = 4$

$\square - 3 = 1$

$4 - \square = 3$

Bonus:

Can you make two family facts of your own?

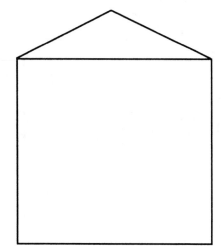

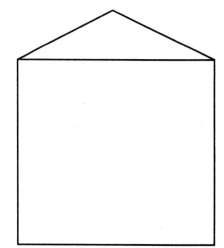

Family Facts Fiesta

Complete the families of math facts.

$\square$ + 4 = 5

1 + 4 = $\square$

5 - $\square$ = 4

$\square$ - 4 = 1

6 - $\square$ = 3

$\square$ - 3 = 3

3 + 3 = $\square$

$\square$ + 3 = 6

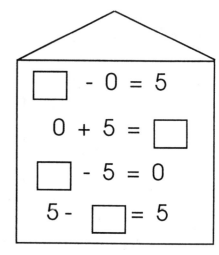

$\square$ - 0 = 5

0 + 5 = $\square$

$\square$ - 5 = 0

5 - $\square$ = 5

$\square$ + 0 = 4

$\square$ + 4 = 4

4 - $\square$ = 0

4 - 4 = $\square$

2 + $\square$ = 4

4 - 2 = $\square$

4 - $\square$ = 2

$\square$ - 2 = 2

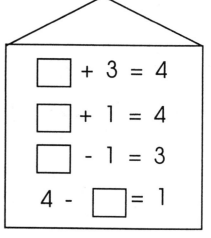

$\square$ + 3 = 4

$\square$ + 1 = 4

$\square$ - 1 = 3

4 - $\square$ = 1

Bonus:

Can you make two family facts of your own?

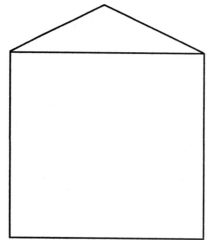

Hopscotch

Use your math facts to complete the hopscotch board.

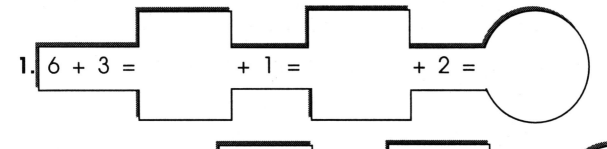

1. 6 + 3 =   + 1 =   + 2 =

2. 4 + 5 =   + 1 =   + 1 =

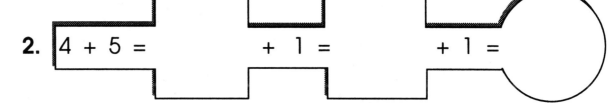

3. 6 + 4 =   + 1 =   + 0 =

4. 5 + 2 =   + 3 =   + 2 =

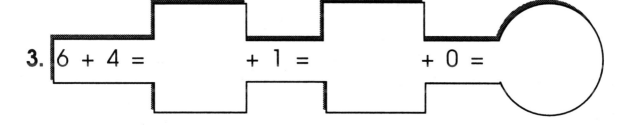

5. 8 + 0 =   + 0 =   + 1 =

6. 4 + 2 =   + 2 =   + 4 =

Cross Challenge

Draw a line from a math expression in Column A to the number it equals in Column B. The first problem is done for you. In the boxes under Column C, draw the correct number of balls for each number.

<u>Column A</u>   <u>Column B</u>   <u>Column C</u>

$4 + 4$ o ————————————————— o 1

$0 + 2$ o   o 2

$3 + 3$ o   o 3

$6 + 6$ o   o 4

$5 + 4$ o   o 5

$4 + 0$ o   o 6

$3 + 4$ o   o 7

$6 + 4$ o   o 8

$2 + 3$ o   o 9

$7 + 4$ o   o 10

$1 + 2$ o   o 11

$1 + 0$ o   o 12

Mystery Math

Look at the mystery number. Circle all math expressions in that row which equal the mystery number. The first problem is done for you.

Mystery Number	Math Expression			
9	2 + 6	(6 + 3)	(4 + 5)	(1 + 8)
6	1 + 5	3 + 4	3 + 3	4 + 2
11	6 + 6	8 + 3	7 + 4	3 + 9
7	5 + 2	3 + 4	4 + 5	6 + 3
5	3 + 1	4 + 2	3 + 2	4 + 1
8	4 + 4	6 + 3	5 + 3	7 + 1
4	1 + 2	2 + 3	3 + 1	2 + 2
10	8 + 2	6 + 4	5 + 5	7 + 3
12	7 + 4	8 + 4	6 + 5	9 + 3

Leapfrog

Use your math facts to move across the lily pads.

1. 2 + 7 = $\bigcirc$ + 3 = $\bigcirc$

2. 5 + 4 = $\bigcirc$ + 2 = $\bigcirc$

3. 4 + 3 = $\bigcirc$ + 5 = $\bigcirc$

4. 6 + 2 = $\bigcirc$ + 2 = $\bigcirc$

5. 6 + 5 = $\bigcirc$ + 1 = $\bigcirc$

6. 4 + 4 = $\bigcirc$ + 3 = $\bigcirc$

7. 5 + 2 = $\bigcirc$ + 4 = $\bigcirc$

8. 3 + 4 = $\bigcirc$ + 3 = $\bigcirc$

9. 6 + 2 = $\bigcirc$ + 3 = $\bigcirc$

10. 3 + 7 = $\bigcirc$ + 2 = $\bigcirc$

Bonus

$$\begin{array}{r} 5 \\ + \ 3 \\ \hline \square \end{array}$$

$$\begin{array}{r} + \ 2 \\ \hline \square \end{array}$$

$$\begin{array}{r} + \ 2 \\ \hline \square \end{array}$$

Fact Finder

Solve each math sentence in the Facts Box. Search the puzzle for facts.
Circle the whole math sentence when you find it.

FACTS BOX

6 + 5 = ____   7 + 5 = ____   6 + 6 = ____

9 + 3 = ____   6 + 4 = ____   6 + 3 = ____

2 + 8 = ____   7 + 4 = ____   8 + 4 = ____

8 + 3 = ____

6	+	12	+	9	+	12	6
+	12	=	5	+	7	14	+
8	+	3	+	8	10	=	6
+	12	+	+	0	=	17	=
3	=	9	8	+	4	=	12
=	5	=	+	5	+	+	13
11	=	4	+	7	6	=	8
8	7	+	2	+	8	=	10
6	+	5	=	11	4	9	=
15	9	16	6	+	3	=	9

Bonus: Did you find a false math fact in the puzzle? Draw a red box around it.

Blankety- Blanks

Solve the problems below and write the answer in the box. On the blanket,
shade in all the numbers that are in the answer boxes.
The answers will make a pattern.

$8 + 4 = \boxed{}$

$\boxed{} + 4 = 12$

$7 + \boxed{} = 11$

$3 + \boxed{} = 9$

$2 + 9 = \boxed{}$

$\boxed{} + 3 = 10$

$\boxed{} + 9 = 12$

$\boxed{} + 6 = 11$

$6 + 4 = \boxed{}$

$1 + 1 = \boxed{}$

$\boxed{} + 1 = 1$

$4 + 5 = \boxed{}$

1	15		12
	11	4	
18	19	14	20
	6	3	
0	13	19	16
	18	17	
16	7	2	13
	20	14	
10	9	5	8
	16		

Compare Sums

Compare the number sentences. Circle the expression that is larger. If they are equal, circle them both. The first problem is done for you.

1. 3 + 6   and   (8 + 2)   11. 6 + 2   and   9 + 0

2. 8 + 3   and   5 + 4   12. 4 + 4   and   6 + 2

3. 5 + 5   and   4 + 6   13. 7 + 5   and   6 + 4

4. 3 + 7   and   4 + 5   14. 8 + 2   and   7 + 4

5. 2 + 7   and   6 + 5   15. 4 + 5   and   8 + 3

6. 5 + 4   and   3 + 6   16. 1 + 6   and   5 + 3

7. 9 + 2   and   5 + 7   17. 5 + 3   and   7 + 2

8. 3 + 6   and   5 + 5   18. 4 + 8   and   6 + 6

9. 3 + 5   and   4 + 5   19. 7 + 3   and   5 + 4

10. 2 + 7   and   5 + 6   20. 8 + 1   and   6 + 3

Name_____ Skill: Addition Facts to 12

Beat the Clock

How quickly can you complete this page? Time yourself. Ready, set, go!

$$
\begin{array}{r} 6 \\ +3 \\ \hline \end{array}
\qquad
\begin{array}{r} 5 \\ +5 \\ \hline \end{array}
\qquad
\begin{array}{r} 8 \\ +2 \\ \hline \end{array}
\qquad
\begin{array}{r} 6 \\ +5 \\ \hline \end{array}
\qquad
\begin{array}{r} 4 \\ +4 \\ \hline \end{array}
$$

$$
\begin{array}{r} 6 \\ +4 \\ \hline \end{array}
\qquad
\begin{array}{r} 3 \\ +8 \\ \hline \end{array}
\qquad
\begin{array}{r} 9 \\ +3 \\ \hline \end{array}
\qquad
\begin{array}{r} 7 \\ +3 \\ \hline \end{array}
\qquad
\begin{array}{r} 8 \\ +1 \\ \hline \end{array}
$$

$$
\begin{array}{r} 9 \\ +1 \\ \hline \end{array}
\qquad
\begin{array}{r} 7 \\ +4 \\ \hline \end{array}
\qquad
\begin{array}{r} 4 \\ +8 \\ \hline \end{array}
\qquad
\begin{array}{r} 2 \\ +9 \\ \hline \end{array}
\qquad
\begin{array}{r} 6 \\ +6 \\ \hline \end{array}
$$

4 + 3 =   5 + 2 =   9 + 0 =

2 + 6 =   4 + 5 =   5 + 7 =

5 + 3 =   1 + 6 =   7 + 2 =

Time : _____
Number Correct : _____

Blankety- Blanks

Solve the problems below and write the answer in the box. On the blanket,
shade in all the numbers that are in the answer boxes.
The answers will make a pattern.

8 - 4 = ☐

☐ - 4 = 7

11 - ☐ = 2

10 - ☐ = 0

10 - 2 = ☐

☐ - 3 = 3

☐ - 3 = 9

☐ - 3 = 2

9 - 8 = ☐

11 - 9 = ☐

☐ - 2 = 1

10 - 3 = ☐

14	7		0
	19	6	
18	11	14	20
	15	3	
12	5	19	4
	18	10	
16	1	16	13
	20	8	
17	2	0	18
	9		

Hopscotch

Use your math facts to complete the hopscotch board.

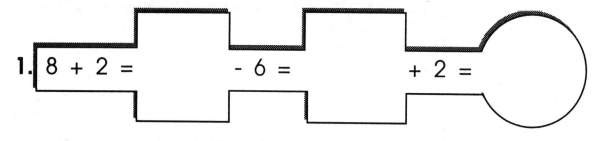

1. | 8 + 2 =   - 6 =   + 2 =

2. | 4 - 4 =   + 1 =   + 4 =

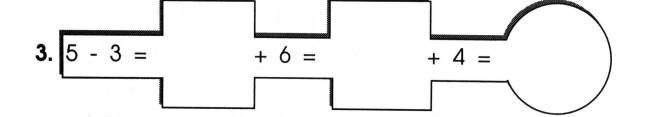

3. | 5 - 3 =   + 6 =   + 4 =

4. | 10 + 2 =   - 6 =   - 6 =

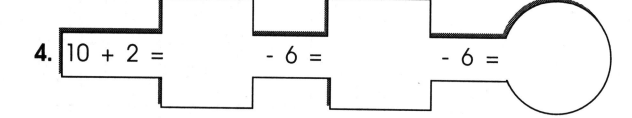

5. | 8 + 4 =   - 3 =   - 1 =

6. | 7 + 1 =   + 4 =   + 0 =

 CD-3721

Cross Challenge

Draw a line from a math expression in Column A to the number it equals in Column B. The first problem is done for you. In the boxes under Column C, draw the correct number of X's for each number.

Column A		Column B	Column C
12 - 6	o	o 0	
12 - 2	o	o 1	
9 - 8	o	o 2	
11 - 6	o	o 3	
12 - 4	o	o 4	
8 - 5	o	o 5	
11 - 2	o	o 6	
12 - 1	o	o 7	
8 - 8	o	o 8	
9 - 5	o	o 9	
10 - 8	o	o 10	
10 - 3	o	o 11	

35 CD-3721

Compare Differences

Compare the number sentences. Circle the expression that is larger. If they are equal, circle them both. The first problem is done for you.

1. 12 - 8   and   (9 - 2)

2. 8 - 3   and   9 - 6

3. 10 - 5   and   12 - 4

4. 11 - 3   and   9 - 2

5. 9 - 4   and   11 - 3

6. 12 - 4   and   9 - 3

7. 10 - 6   and   8 - 4

8. 9 - 5   and   10 - 3

9. 8 - 5   and   9 - 3

10. 7 - 4   and   11 - 8

11. 11 - 7   and   6 - 4

12. 10 - 4   and   7 - 2

13. 9 - 5   and   8 - 4

14. 10 - 2   and   11 - 3

15. 11 - 5   and   8 - 3

16. 9 - 3   and   10 - 5

17. 12 - 3   and   10 - 6

18. 8 - 3   and   10 - 4

19. 11 - 8   and   9 - 6

20. 10 - 7   and   9 - 5

Mystery Math

Look at the mystery number. Circle all math expressions in that row which equal the mystery number. The first problem is done for you.

Mystery Number	Math Expression			
9	12 - 6	(12 - 3)	(10 - 1)	9 - 1
6	11 - 5	10 - 4	9 - 2	8 - 3
2	9 - 7	8 - 5	11 - 9	7 - 3
7	11 - 5	10 - 4	12 - 5	9 - 2
5	10 - 5	9 - 4	11 - 7	12 - 8
8	9 - 2	10 - 3	11 - 3	12 - 4
4	8 - 4	10 - 7	9 - 5	11 - 6
1	10 - 8	8 - 7	6 - 2	7 - 6
3	10 - 7	12 - 9	9 - 6	11 - 7

Leapfrog

Use your math facts to move across the lily pads.

1. 12 - 5 = $\bigcirc$ - 6 = $\bigcirc$

2. 11 - 9 = $\bigcirc$ - 1 = $\bigcirc$

3. 10 - 3 = $\bigcirc$ - 4 = $\bigcirc$

4. 9 - 5 = $\bigcirc$ - 2 = $\bigcirc$

5. 11 - 2 = $\bigcirc$ - 4 = $\bigcirc$

6. 12 - 3 = $\bigcirc$ - 3 = $\bigcirc$

7. 11 - 7 = $\bigcirc$ - 2 = $\bigcirc$

8. 10 - 5 = $\bigcirc$ - 4 = $\bigcirc$

9. 9 - 2 = $\bigcirc$ - 2 = $\bigcirc$

10. 12 - 4 = $\bigcirc$ - 5 = $\bigcirc$

Bonus

$$11$$
$$-$$
$$5$$

$$-$$
$$4$$

$$-$$
$$2$$

38   CD-3721

Blankety- Blanks

Solve the problems below and write the answer in the box. On the blanket, shade in all the numbers that are in the answer boxes.
The answers will make a pattern.

9 - 3 = ☐

☐ - 6 = 6

10 - ☐ = 2

12 - ☐ = 3

10 - 6 = ☐

☐ - 2 = 1

☐ - 3 = 8

☐ - 5 = 5

9 - 7 = ☐

11 - 4 = ☐

☐ - 2 = 3

10 - 9 = ☐

14	20	0
	19 · 16	
11	18 · 14	12
	7 · 3	
19	1 · 4	13
	9 · 2	
10	8 · 6	5
	20 · 14	
17	19 · 0	18
	15	

Beat the Clock

How quickly can you complete this page? Time yourself. Ready, set, go!

$$\begin{array}{r} 8 \\ -\ 3 \\ \hline \end{array} \qquad \begin{array}{r} 9 \\ -\ 4 \\ \hline \end{array} \qquad \begin{array}{r} 10 \\ -\ 5 \\ \hline \end{array} \qquad \begin{array}{r} 11 \\ -\ 3 \\ \hline \end{array} \qquad \begin{array}{r} 7 \\ -\ 4 \\ \hline \end{array}$$

$$\begin{array}{r} 12 \\ -\ 9 \\ \hline \end{array} \qquad \begin{array}{r} 10 \\ -\ 6 \\ \hline \end{array} \qquad \begin{array}{r} 12 \\ -\ 3 \\ \hline \end{array} \qquad \begin{array}{r} 11 \\ -\ 5 \\ \hline \end{array} \qquad \begin{array}{r} 10 \\ -\ 8 \\ \hline \end{array}$$

$$\begin{array}{r} 11 \\ -\ 7 \\ \hline \end{array} \qquad \begin{array}{r} 10 \\ -\ 4 \\ \hline \end{array} \qquad \begin{array}{r} 9 \\ -\ 5 \\ \hline \end{array} \qquad \begin{array}{r} 11 \\ -\ 6 \\ \hline \end{array} \qquad \begin{array}{r} 12 \\ -\ 7 \\ \hline \end{array}$$

9 - 6 =   11 - 8 =   8 - 5 =

10 - 7 =   12 - 6 =   11 - 4 =

12 - 5 =   10 - 2 =   11 - 9 =

Time : _____
Number Correct : _____

                   CD-3721

Magic Trail

Follow the trail by solving math problems and find the magic number.

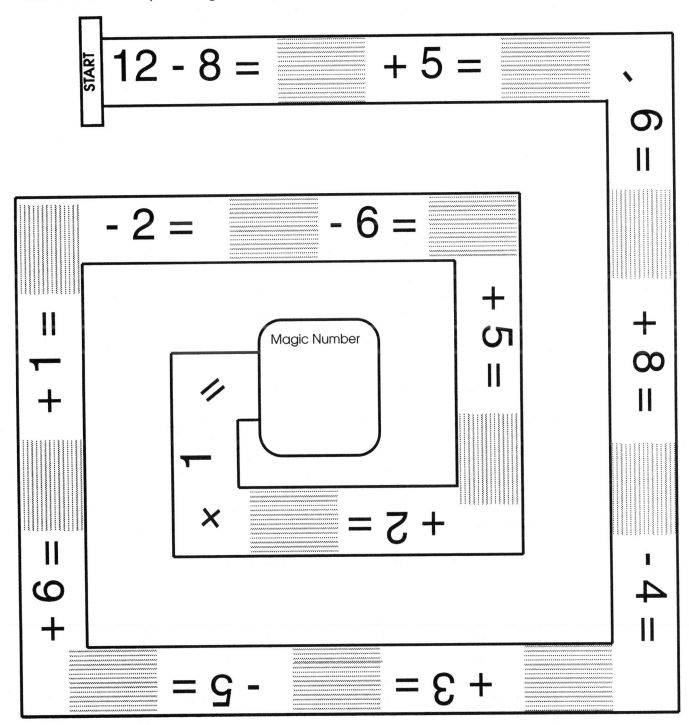

START | 12 - 8 = [____] + 5 = [____]

MAGIC NUMBER _____

Hopscotch

Use your math facts to complete the hopscotch board.

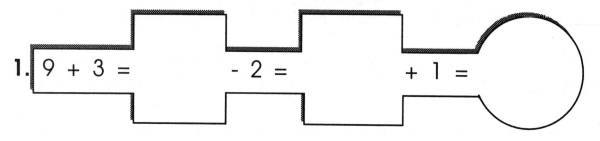

1. 9 + 3 =   - 2 =   + 1 =

2. 8 + 2 =   - 3 =   + 1 =

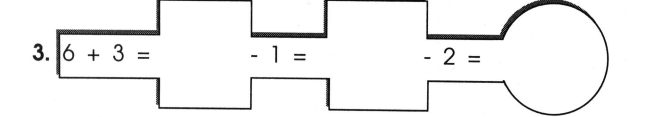

3. 6 + 3 =   - 1 =   - 2 =

4. 9 - 3 =   - 3 =   - 1 =

5. 8 + 1 =   - 3 =   + 1 =

6. 7 + 1 =   - 2 =   + 1 =

CD-3721

Cross Challenge

Draw a line from a math expression in Column A to the number it equals in Column B. The first problem is done for you. In the boxes under Column C, draw the correct number of X's for each number.

Column A   Column B   Column C

12 - 6   ○   0

12 - 2   ○   ○   1

9 - 8   ○   ○   2

11 - 6   ○   ○   3

12 - 4   ○   ○   4

8 - 5   ○   ○   5

11 - 2   ○   ○   6

12 - 1   ○   ○   7

8 - 8   ○   ○   8

9 - 5   ○   ○   9

10 - 8   ○   ○   10

10 - 3   ○   ○   11

Compare Equations

Compare the number sentences. Circle the expression that is larger. If they are equal, circle them both. The first problem is done for you.

1. 11 - 4   and $\boxed{8 + 4}$

2. 10 - 6   and   2 + 4

3. 9 - 3   and   5 + 3

4. 11 - 3   and   12 - 5

5. 6 + 5   and   12 - 3

6. 4 + 4   and   11 - 3

7. 7 + 2   and   10 - 2

8. 12 - 6   and   2 + 5

9. 10 - 5   and   4 + 6

10. 7 + 3   and   2 + 9

11. 12 - 0   and   6 + 5

12. 10 - 7   and   2 + 1

13. 9 + 3   and   6 + 6

14. 7 - 2   and   3 + 4

15. 3 + 3   and   12 - 7

16. 4 + 5   and   11 - 5

17. 12 - 8   and   0 + 5

18. 4 + 7   and   8 + 2

19. 12 - 5   and   2 + 5

20. 11 - 3   and   5 + 3

Blankety- Blanks

Solve the problems below and write the answer in the box. On the blanket, shade in all the numbers that are in the answer boxes.
The answers will make a pattern.

9 + 3 = ☐

☐ - 6 = 1

10 - ☐ = 9

3 + ☐ = 11

10 - 4 = ☐

☐ - 6 = 5

☐ + 3 = 7

☐ + 7 = 10

12 - 7 = ☐

8 + 2 = ☐

☐ - 2 = 7

6 - 4 = ☐

	11		
4	19	16	6
1	18	14	12
	17	13	
9	0	14	3
	19	20	
10	18	16	2
	20	14	
7	19	0	8
	5		

CD-3721

Family Facts Fiesta

Complete the families of math facts.

☐ - 9 = 3	6 + ☐ = 11	☐ + 8 = 12
12 - 3 = ☐	☐ + 5 = 11	4 + ☐ = 12
9 + 3 = ☐	11 - 5 = ☐	☐ - 8 = 4
☐ + 9 = 12	11 - 6 = ☐	12 - ☐ = 8

☐ + 5 = 9	7 + ☐ = 10	☐ + 6 = 9
4 + 5 = ☐	10 - 7 = ☐	6 + 3 = ☐
9 - ☐ = 4	3 + ☐ = 10	9 - 6 = ☐
☐ - 4 = 5	☐ - 3 = 7	9 - ☐ = 6

Bonus:

Can you make two family facts of your own?

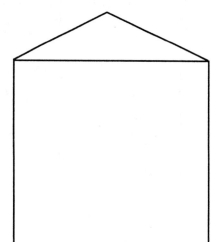

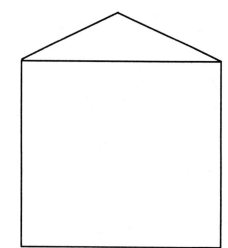

Family Facts Fiesta

Complete the families of math facts.

□ + 4 = 11
7 + □ = 11
11 - □ = 4
□ - 4 = 7

5 + □ = 10
□ - 5 = 5
5 + 5 = □
10 - □ = 5

□ + 3 = 8
3 + 5 = □
□ - 3 = 5
8 - □ = 3

7 + □ = 12
5 + 7 = □
12 - □ = 5
□ - 5 = 7

8 + □ = 11
3 + 8 = □
11 - □ = 3
□ - 3 = 8

□ + 2 = 9
2 + 7 = □
□ - 7 = 2
9 - □ = 7

Bonus:

Can you make two family facts of your own?

I'm thinking of a number....

Read the clues and write the numbers in the proper place on the grid.

1. I'm thinking of a number with a 3 in the hundreds place, a 2 in the ones place, and a 4 in the tens place.
What is the number?

$$\overline{}\quad\overline{}\quad\overline{}$$
H   T   O

2. I'm thinking of a number with a 6 in the ones place, a 2 in the the tens place and a 7 in the hundreds place.
What is the number?

$$\overline{}\quad\overline{}\quad\overline{}$$
H   T   O

3. I'm thinking of a number with a 2 in the ones place, an 8 in the tens place, and a 3 in the hundreds place.
What is the number?

$$\overline{}\quad\overline{}\quad\overline{}$$
H   T   O

4. I'm thinking of a number with a 9 in the tens place, a 4 in the ones place, and a 1 in the hundreds place.
What is the number?

$$\overline{}\quad\overline{}\quad\overline{}$$
H   T   O

5. I'm thinking of a number with a 5 in the tens place, a 2 in the hundreds place, and a 7 in the ones place.
What is the number?

$$\overline{}\quad\overline{}\quad\overline{}$$
H   T   O

I' m thinking of a number....

Read the clues and write the numbers in the proper place on the grid.

1. I'm thinking of a number with a 5 in the ones place, a 1 in the tens place, and a 3 in the hundreds place.
What is the number?

$$\overline{} \quad \overline{} \quad \overline{}$$
H   T   O

2. I'm thinking of a number with an 8 in the tens place, a 4 in the hundreds place, and a 9 in the ones place.
What is the number?

$$\overline{} \quad \overline{} \quad \overline{}$$
H   T   O

3. I'm thinking of a number with a 2 in the tens place, a 6 in the hundreds place, and a 4 in the ones place.
What is the number?

$$\overline{} \quad \overline{} \quad \overline{}$$
H   T   O

4. I'm thinking of a number with a 3 in the ones place, a 2 in the tens place, and a 7 in the hundreds place.
What is the number?

$$\overline{} \quad \overline{} \quad \overline{}$$
H   T   O

5. I'm thinking of a number with a 3 in the ones and tens places, and a 6 in the hundreds place.
What is the number?

$$\overline{} \quad \overline{} \quad \overline{}$$
H   T   O

Name _____   Skill: Place Value to Hundreds

Which Digit?

Read the problems carefully. Answer the questions.

1. The number is **423**.

    A. Which digit is in the hundreds place? _____
    B. Which digit is in the tens place? _____
    C. Which digit is in the ones place? _____

2. The number is **201**.

    A. Which digit is in the tens place? _____
    B. Which digit is in the hundreds place? _____
    C. Which digit is in the ones place? _____

3. The number is **126**.

    A. Which digit is in the tens place? _____
    B. Which digit is in the hundreds place? _____
    C. Which digit is in the ones place? _____

4. The number is **314**.

    A. Which digit is in the ones place? _____
    B. Which digit is in the hundreds place? _____
    C. Which digit is in the tens? _____

4. The number is **541**.

    A. Which digit is in the ones place? _____
    B. Which digit is in the hundreds place? _____
    C. Which digit is in the tens? _____

Place Value Polka

Read the problems carefully then name the new numbers.

1. The number is **114**.

    A. Name the number that is 10 more. _____
    B. Name the number that is 100 less. _____
    C. Name the number that is 10 less. _____
    D. Name the number that is 1 more. _____

2. The number is **356**.

    A. Name the number that is 1 less. _____
    B. Name the number that is 100 more. _____
    C. Name the number that is 10 less. _____
    D. Name the number that is 10 more. _____

3. The number is **473**.

    A. Name the number that is 10 less. _____
    B. Name the number that is 100 less. _____
    C. Name the number that is 100 more. _____
    D. Name the number that is 1 more. _____

4. The number is **225**.

    A. Name the number that is 10 more. _____
    B. Name the number that is 100 less. _____
    C. Name the number that is 1 less. _____
    D. Name the number that is 10 less. _____

Place Value Polka

Read the problems carefully then name the new numbers.

1. The number is **678**.

    A. Name the number that is 100 less. _____
    B. Name the number that is 100 more. _____
    C. Name the number that is 10 more. _____
    D. Name the number that is 10 less. _____

2. The number is **306**.

    A. Name the number that is 100 more. _____
    B. Name the number that is 100 less. _____
    C. Name the number that is 10 more. _____
    D. Name the number that is 1 more. _____

3. The number is **421**.

    A. Name the number that is 1 less. _____
    B. Name the number that is 10 more. _____
    C. Name the number that is 100 less. _____
    D. Name the number that is 100 more. _____

4. The number is **294**.

    A. Name the number that is 100 more. _____
    B. Name the number that is 100 less. _____
    C. Name the number that is 10 less. _____
    D. Name the number that is 1 more. _____

Compare Numbers

Compare the number sentences. Circle the expression that is larger. If they are equal, circle them both. The first problem is done for you.

1. 600 and (700)

2. 200 and 300

3. 500 and 600

4. 800 and 700

5. 100 and 200

6. 800 and 600

7. 900 and 600

8. 300 and 400

9. 200 and 200

10. 400 and 500

11. 199 and 200

12. 400 and 395

13. 305 and 295

14. 615 and 590

15. 125 and 210

16. 460 and 520

17. 825 and 725

18. 450 and 430

19. 575 and 560

20. 355 and 375

Compare Numbers

Compare the number sentences. Circle the expression that is larger. If they are equal, circle them both. The first problem is done for you.

1. 456	and	(465)	**11.** 413	and	431
2. 219	and	291	**12.** 770	and	707
3. 117	and	711	**13.** 564	and	546
4. 531	and	351	**14.** 988	and	988
5. 222	and	221	**15.** 315	and	331
6. 405	and	399	**16.** 664	and	464
7. 638	and	683	**17.** 235	and	325
8. 109	and	110	**18.** 115	and	151
9. 274	and	472	**19.** 234	and	156
10. 689	and	986	**20.** 133	and	313

Adding Two-Digit Numbers

30 + 20	70 + 10	20 + 50	70 + 20	40 + 30
50 + 20	30 + 40	20 + 70	60 + 10	50 + 40
61 + 30	43 + 40	86 + 10	24 + 60	74 + 10
77 + 20	23 + 30	36 + 30	63 + 20	21 + 40

10 + 10 =   20 + 20 =   30 + 40 =   50 + 40 =

16 + 30 =   50 + 11 =   48 + 20 =   70 + 14 =

31 + 18 =   22 + 44 =   75 + 14 =   43 + 33 =

Adding Two-Digit Numbers

30	40	20	70	70
+ 20	+ 30	+ 40	+ 20	+ 10

50	50	20	60	30
+ 20	+ 40	+ 30	+ 10	+ 40

61	74	86	24	43
+ 30	+ 10	+ 10	+ 60	+ 40

77	21	36	63	23
+ 20	+ 40	+ 30	+ 20	+ 30

35 + 20 =   64 + 21 =   33 + 54 =   12 + 24 =

10 + 22 =   30 + 17 =   28 + 30 =   42 + 35 =

41 + 12 =   23 + 40 =   45 + 22 =   15 + 12 =

Adding Two-Digit Numbers

27 + 41	25 + 30	66 + 22	42 + 37	40 + 35
50 + 39	24 + 54	15 + 43	42 + 33	53 + 21
50 + 36	41 + 28	23 + 46	17 + 40	76 + 22
70 + 16	36 + 23	36 + 30	54 + 32	15 + 14

30 + 23 =   47 + 21 =   22 + 54 =   80 + 12 =

13 + 64 =   24 + 61 =   30 + 55 =   55 + 14 =

43 + 15 =   42 + 27 =   21 + 20 =   14 + 51 =

Adding 3 Digit Numbers

300 + 400	400 + 100	300 + 200	700 + 100	500 + 300
500 + 100	300 + 600	200 + 400	800 + 100	200 + 200
550 + 230	420 + 460	560 + 320	280 + 410	170 + 520
585 + 110	132 + 163	347 + 131	397 + 202	723 + 223

200 + 590 =   250 + 300 =   470 + 100 =

530 + 250 =   350 + 409 =   240 + 445 =

518 + 270 =   277 + 111 =   363 + 125 =

Adding 3 Digit Numbers

200 + 100	500 + 200	600 + 300	300 + 400	200 + 100
400 + 300	200 + 400	300 + 500	200 + 500	100 + 100
420 + 220	520 + 320	620 + 230	456 + 312	350 + 320
505 + 310	242 + 253	525 + 132	406 + 321	625 + 333

300 + 450 =   540 + 355 =   350 + 220 =

230 + 330 =   650 + 341 =   225 + 311 =

418 + 230 =   127 + 451 =   320 + 355 =

Adding 3 Digit Numbers

326 + 322	132 + 231	438 + 250	345 + 220	407 + 131
574 + 222	534 + 400	325 + 460	561 + 312	525 + 272
602 + 233	240 + 439	582 + 115	140 + 140	626 + 133
770 + 105	123 + 643	376 + 313	631 + 257	813 + 142

260 + 103 =   421 + 255 =   340 + 401 =

435 + 122 =   533 + 130 =   455 + 244 =

615 + 132 =   327 + 221 =   306 + 103 =

Subtracting 2 Digit Numbers

$$
\begin{array}{r} 30 \\ -\,20 \\ \hline \end{array}
\qquad
\begin{array}{r} 70 \\ -\,10 \\ \hline \end{array}
\qquad
\begin{array}{r} 80 \\ -\,50 \\ \hline \end{array}
\qquad
\begin{array}{r} 70 \\ -\,30 \\ \hline \end{array}
\qquad
\begin{array}{r} 40 \\ -\,30 \\ \hline \end{array}
$$

$$
\begin{array}{r} 50 \\ -\,40 \\ \hline \end{array}
\qquad
\begin{array}{r} 40 \\ -\,20 \\ \hline \end{array}
\qquad
\begin{array}{r} 60 \\ -\,50 \\ \hline \end{array}
\qquad
\begin{array}{r} 60 \\ -\,10 \\ \hline \end{array}
\qquad
\begin{array}{r} 50 \\ -\,20 \\ \hline \end{array}
$$

$$
\begin{array}{r} 69 \\ -\,30 \\ \hline \end{array}
\qquad
\begin{array}{r} 55 \\ -\,30 \\ \hline \end{array}
\qquad
\begin{array}{r} 83 \\ -\,10 \\ \hline \end{array}
\qquad
\begin{array}{r} 92 \\ -\,50 \\ \hline \end{array}
\qquad
\begin{array}{r} 78 \\ -\,10 \\ \hline \end{array}
$$

$$
\begin{array}{r} 78 \\ -\,10 \\ \hline \end{array}
\qquad
\begin{array}{r} 99 \\ -\,20 \\ \hline \end{array}
\qquad
\begin{array}{r} 88 \\ -\,20 \\ \hline \end{array}
\qquad
\begin{array}{r} 65 \\ -\,20 \\ \hline \end{array}
\qquad
\begin{array}{r} 86 \\ -\,40 \\ \hline \end{array}
$$

20 - 10 =   40 - 20 =   80 - 40 =   70 - 40 =

86 - 30 =   55 - 10 =   68 - 10 =   71 - 30 =

34 - 10 =   67 - 40 =   77 - 10 =   49 - 30 =

Subtracting 2 Digit Numbers

$$
\begin{array}{r} 98 \\ -27 \\ \hline \end{array}
\qquad
\begin{array}{r} 66 \\ -43 \\ \hline \end{array}
\qquad
\begin{array}{r} 89 \\ -38 \\ \hline \end{array}
\qquad
\begin{array}{r} 78 \\ -37 \\ \hline \end{array}
\qquad
\begin{array}{r} 43 \\ -21 \\ \hline \end{array}
$$

$$
\begin{array}{r} 75 \\ -54 \\ \hline \end{array}
\qquad
\begin{array}{r} 94 \\ -23 \\ \hline \end{array}
\qquad
\begin{array}{r} 68 \\ -36 \\ \hline \end{array}
\qquad
\begin{array}{r} 68 \\ -12 \\ \hline \end{array}
\qquad
\begin{array}{r} 54 \\ -31 \\ \hline \end{array}
$$

$$
\begin{array}{r} 84 \\ -22 \\ \hline \end{array}
\qquad
\begin{array}{r} 27 \\ -15 \\ \hline \end{array}
\qquad
\begin{array}{r} 78 \\ -45 \\ \hline \end{array}
\qquad
\begin{array}{r} 95 \\ -54 \\ \hline \end{array}
\qquad
\begin{array}{r} 76 \\ -15 \\ \hline \end{array}
$$

$$
\begin{array}{r} 76 \\ -43 \\ \hline \end{array}
\qquad
\begin{array}{r} 96 \\ -76 \\ \hline \end{array}
\qquad
\begin{array}{r} 88 \\ -57 \\ \hline \end{array}
\qquad
\begin{array}{r} 48 \\ -23 \\ \hline \end{array}
\qquad
\begin{array}{r} 69 \\ -44 \\ \hline \end{array}
$$

$49 - 27 =$ $59 - 25 =$ $87 - 37 =$ $65 - 13 =$

$81 - 41 =$ $57 - 34 =$ $62 - 11 =$ $77 - 34 =$

$37 - 21 =$ $68 - 32 =$ $79 - 53 =$ $43 - 21 =$

                   CD-3721

Subtracting 2 Digit Numbers

65	76	99	52	66
- 32	- 53	- 33	- 41	- 42

55	98	45	68	65
- 21	- 31	- 23	- 21	- 44

99	78	59	84	87
- 35	- 12	- 45	- 24	- 25

56	35	79	58	74
- 23	- 21	- 42	- 41	- 21

48 - 26 =   58 - 35 =   67 - 36 =   74 - 10 =

71 - 40 =   55 - 33 =   52 - 12 =   78 - 33 =

67 - 23 =   78 - 52 =   69 - 43 =   33 - 22 =

Subtracting 2 Digit Numbers

68	63	91	88	42
- 51	- 63	- 30	- 36	- 31

54	54	79	98	44
- 21	- 13	- 30	- 32	- 33

46	48	65	45	56
- 12	- 13	- 22	- 24	- 14

87	78	45	21	60
- 65	- 45	- 14	- 11	- 40

59 - 31 =   66 - 35 =   94 - 33 =   78 - 15 =

71 - 21 =   77 - 64 =   65 - 21 =   87 - 32 =

57 - 31 =   88 - 52 =   71 - 50 =   53 - 22 =

Subtracting 3 Digit Numbers

250	500	300	800	600
- 100	- 400	- 100	- 500	- 300

700	800	500	700	500
- 400	- 100	- 200	- 400	- 400

550	760	680	670	560
- 350	- 530	- 270	- 340	- 120

680	340	560	530	980
- 270	- 220	- 430	- 310	- 710

300 - 200 =   480 - 320 =   800 - 400 =

650 - 130 =   670 - 470 =   570 - 340 =

790 - 160 =   380 - 150 =   650 - 340 =

Subtracting 3 Digit Numbers

500 - 100	800 - 700	850 - 330	440 - 120	300 - 200
600 - 400	400 - 200	650 - 420	620 - 200	500 - 400
570 - 330	580 - 260	870 - 250	505 - 105	410 - 310
650 - 320	370 - 250	360 - 210	790 - 320	450 - 230

400 - 300 =   320 - 110 =   650 - 420 =

650 - 150 =   250 - 130 =   430 - 320 =

670 - 160 =   460 - 130 =   540 - 340 =

Subtracting 3 Digit Numbers

300 - 200	900 - 600	400 - 200	300 - 100	400 - 100
800 - 500	600 - 400	800 - 400	500 - 300	700 - 200
630 - 230	640 - 430	590 - 180	250 - 140	480 - 110
780 - 170	420 - 110	490 - 330	630 - 220	810 - 610

200 - 100 =   400 - 200 =   800 - 700 =

430 - 120 =   580 - 180 =   490 - 240 =

680 - 170 =   360 - 120 =   340 - 140 =

Subtracting 3 Digit Numbers

826	973	843	688	537
- 610	- 650	- 720	- 370	- 430

729	694	875	459	767
- 412	- 453	- 462	- 249	- 253

888	674	564	297	899
- 526	- 341	- 221	- 186	- 487

365	558	846	648	866
- 163	- 223	- 305	- 238	- 242

642 - 330 =   796 - 590 =   843 - 740 =

457 - 236 =   659 - 324 =   485 - 321 =

978 - 267 =   897 - 433 =   774 - 573 =

Words Into Math
Read the paragraph carefully then answer the questions.

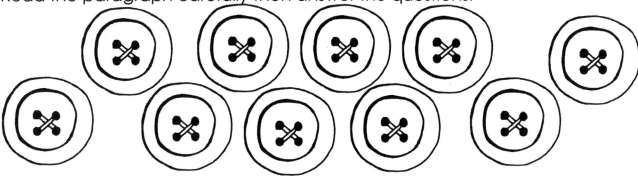

Ray has 10 buttons. He gave 2 buttons to Trey.

1. How many buttons did Ray start with?

_____

2. How many buttons did Ray give to Trey?

_____

3. How many buttons does Ray have left?

_____

4. How many buttons does Trey have now?

_____

5. If Ray loses one button, how many will he have left?

_____

6. How many buttons do Ray and Trey have in all?

_____

7. If Trey finds 7 buttons how many will he have?

_____

8. If the boys give away all the buttons, how many will they have?

_____

Words Into Math

Read the paragraph carefully then answer the questions.

Kara was home. She rode her bicycle 20 miles to the store. She rode 10 more miles to her school.

1. What 2 places did Kara go?

_____

2. How many miles from home to the store?

_____

3. How many miles from the store to school?

_____

4. How many miles did Kara ride all together?

_____

5. How much further is it to school than to the store?

_____

6. How many miles from home to school and home again?

_____

7. How far will Kara ride from school back home?

_____

8. How far is it from the store to school and back to the store?

_____

Words Into Math

Read the paragraph carefully then answer the questions.

Brian is 8 years old. Ben is 2 years older than Brian. Blair is 2 years older than Ben.

1. How old is Brian?

2. How old is Ben?

_____

_____

3. How old is Blair?

4. How much older is Blair than Ben?

_____

_____

5. How much older is Ben than Brian?

6. Who is the oldest boy?

_____

_____

7. Who is the youngest boy?

8. How many years are the boys all together?

_____

_____

CD-3721

Words Into Math

Read the paragraph carefully then answer the questions.

Joe has 3 books about cars, 7 books about dogs, and 3 books about trees.

1. Does Joe have more books about cars or dogs?

_____

2. How many books about dogs and cars all together?

_____

3. How many books does Joe have in all?

_____

4. How many more books about dogs than trees?

_____

5. Which kind of book does Joe have the most of?

_____

6. How many books about trees does Joe have?

_____

7. How many books about trees and cars together?

_____

8. Joe has the same number of which two books?

_____

Words Into Math

Read the paragraph carefully then answer the questions.

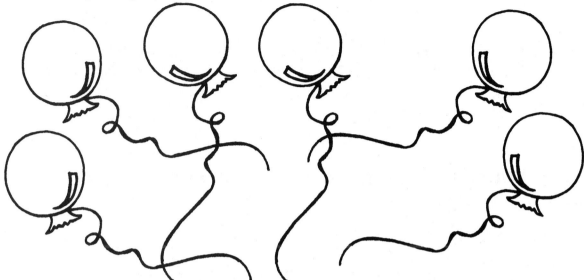

Liz blew up 10 red balloons. Beth blew up 4 yellow balloons. Mari blew up 3 orange balloons.

1. How many girls blew up balloons?

_____

2. How many balloons did Liz and Mari blow up in all?

_____

3. How many balloons did Beth and Mari blow up in all?

_____

4. How many balloons did the girls blow up all together?

_____

5. Who blew up more balloons, Beth or Liz?

_____

6. Who blew up less balloons, Liz or Mari?

_____

Words Into Math

Read the paragraph carefully then answer the questions.

**Kesha has 10 baskets. She filled 4 of them with cookies.
She filled 2 more with toys.**

1. How many baskets does Kesha have?

2. How many baskets are filled with cookies?

_____

3. How many baskets are filled with toys?

4. How many baskets are empty?

_____

5. How many baskets have something in them?

6. Are more baskets filled or empty?

_____

7. Are more baskets full of toys or empty?

8. Are there more baskets with cookies or toys?

_____

Words Into Math

Read the paragraph carefully then answer the questions.

10 birds were sitting on a fence. 3 birds flew to a tree. 2 more flew down to the grass.

1. How many birds were on the fence?

2. How many birds flew to the tree?

_____

3. How many birds flew to the grass?

4. How many birds were left on the fence?

_____

5. Are there more birds on the fence or in the tree?

6. Are there more birds in the grass or the tree?

_____

7. How many birds flew from the fence?

8. How many birds were on the fence and in the grass?

_____

Words Into Math

Read the paragraph carefully then answer the questions.

Amos needs 11 nails. He found 6 nails in the closet. He found 2 more nails in the garage.

1. How many nails does Amos need?

_____

2. How many nails were in the closet?

_____

3. How many nails were in the garage?

_____

4. How many nails were in the closet and the garage?

_____

5. Did Amos find more nails in the closet or garage?

_____

6. How many nails does Amos have now?

_____

7. How many nails does Amos still need?

_____

8. Where did Amos find the fewest nails, in the closet or garage?

_____

Words Into Math

Read the paragraph carefully then answer the questions.

George has some dogs. He has 4 gray ones, 3 black ones, and 2 spotted ones.

1. How many dogs does George have in all?

_____

2. How many dogs are gray?

_____

3. How many dogs are spotted?

_____

4. Are there more black or spotted dogs?

_____

5. How many gray and spotted dogs toether?

_____

6. How many black and gray dogs are there?

_____

7. Are there more black or gray dogs?

_____

8. How many black and spotted dogs are there?

_____

Words Into Math

Read the paragraph carefully then answer the questions.

Welcome To Our Class!

There are 12 children in the first grade class. 8 of the children are boys. 2 are seven years old. The rest are 6 years old.

1. How many children are in the class?

_____

2. How many boys are in the class?

_____

3. How many girls are in the class?

_____

4. Are more children boys or girls?

_____

5. Are more children six or seven years old?

_____

6. How many children are seven years old?

_____

7. How many children are six years old?

_____

8. Are there less boys or girls?

_____

Words Into Math

Read the paragraph carefully then answer the questions.

Rudy has 6 green flowers, 5 red flowers, and 2 white flowers.

1. How many flowers are green?

_____

2. How many flowers are white?

_____

3. How many flowers are red?

_____

4. How many flowers does Rudy have?

_____

5. Are there more red or green flowers?

_____

6. How many green and white flowers in all?

_____

7. How many red and green flowers in all?

_____

8. How many white and red flowers in all?

_____

What Is Next?

Find the pattern in each series below. Draw the next three members of the series on the lines.

1. A B A B A B A B ___ ___ ___

2. A B C A B C A B ___ ___ ___

3. Z Z Y Z Z Y Z Z Y ___ ___ ___

4. A A B B A A B B ___ ___ ___

5. Z O P Z O P Z O ___ ___ ___

6. A A A B B B A A ___ ___ ___

7. S G S G S G S G ___ ___ ___

8. W W T W W T W ___ ___ ___

9. A B A C A B A C ___ ___ ___

10. L M M L M M L M ___ ___ ___

Bonus: Design your own pattern of letters for your class to solve.

What Is Next?

Find the pattern in each series below. Draw the next three members
of the series on the lines.

1. # + # + # + # + ___ ___ ___

2. = = + = = + = = ___ ___ ___

3. (W W (W W (W ___ ___ ___

4. P = # P = # P = ___ ___ ___

5. + O # = + O # = ___ ___ ___

6. F T F F T F T F F ___ ___ ___

7.) # +) # +) # ___ ___ ___

8. H I J H I J H I J ___ ___ ___

Bonus: Design your own pattern for your class to solve.

Name _____

What Is Next?

Find the pattern in each series below. Draw the next three members
of the series on the lines.

1. ☐ ○ ☐ ○ ☐ ○ ☐ ○ ___ ___ ___

2. ○ ○ ☐ ☐ ○ ○ ☐ ☐ ___ ___ ___

3. ○ ○ ○ ☐ ○ ○ ○ ☐ ___ ___ ___

4. ☐ ☐ ◯ ☐ ☐ ◯ ☐ ☐ ___ ___ ___

5. ○ ○ ☐ ☐ ☐ ○ ○ ☐ ___ ___ ___

6. ○ ☐ ○ ☐ ○ ☐ ○ ___ ___ ___

7. ☐ ☐ ☐ ☐ ☐ ☐ ☐ ☐ ___ ___ ___

8. ⊟ ☐ ⊟ ☐ ⊟ ☐ ⊟ ___ ___ ___

Bonus: Design your own pattern of shapes for your class to solve.

What Is Next?

Find the pattern in each series below. Draw the next three members of the series on the lines.

1. (( )) # # ((___ ___ ___

2. (%) % (%) % ___ ___ ___

3. 0 0 0 ⊂⊃ 0 0 0 ⊂⊃ ___ ___ ___

4. ✔ ✕ ✕ ✔ ✕ ✔ ✕ ✕ ___ ___ ___

5. ▯▯ ▤ ▭ ▤ ▯▯ ▤ ▭ ▯▯ ▤ ___ ___ ___

6. ⊖ ⊘ ⊖ ⊘ ⊖ ⊘ ⊖ ⊘ ___ ___ ___

7. ★ ★ ★ ☆ ★ ★ ★ ☆ ___ ___ ___

8. ◆ ◆ ◆ ✱ ✱ ◆ ◆ ◆ ✱ ___ ___ ___

Bonus: Design your own pattern for your class to solve.

Name _____

What Is Next?

Find the pattern in each series below. Draw the next three members
of the series on the lines.

1.   1,   2,   1,   2,   1,   ___ ___ ___

2.   10,   20,   10,   20,   10,   ___ ___ ___

3.   1,   2,   3,   1,   2,   3,   ___ ___ ___

4.   3,   4,   5,   3,   4,   5,   ___ ___ ___

5.   1,   10,   10,   1,   10,   ___ ___ ___

6.   1,   2,   3,   4,   5,   ___ ___ ___

7.   2,   4,   6,   8,   10,   ___ ___ ___

8.   1,   11,   2,   12,   3,   ___ ___ ___

Bonus: Design your own pattern of numerals for your class to solve.

What Is Next?

Find the pattern in each series below. Draw the next three members of the series on the lines.

1.   1,   10,   2,   20,   3,   ___ ___ ___

2.   1,   11,   2,   22,   3,   ___ ___ ___

3.   1,   2,   10,   20,   1,   2,   ___ ___ ___

4.   10,   9,   8,   7,   6,   5,   ___ ___ ___

5.   1,   2,   3,   1,   2,   3,   ___ ___ ___

6.   11,   22,   11,   22,   11,   ___ ___ ___

7.   3,   2,   1,   3,   2,   1,   ___ ___ ___

8.   4,   5,   44,   55,   4,   5,   ___ ___ ___

Bonus: Design your own pattern of numerals for your class to solve.

Name _____

What Is Next?

Find the pattern in each series below. Draw the next three members
of the series on the lines.

1. 1,   1,   2,   1,   1,   2,   ___ ___ ___

2. 8,   7,   6,   5,   4,   ___ ___ ___

3. 80,   70,   60,   50,   40,   ___ ___ ___

4. 800, 700, 600, 500, 400, ___ ___ ___

5. 1,   2,   3,   4,   5,   ___ ___ ___

6. 10,   20,   30,   40,   50,   ___ ___ ___

7. 100, 200, 300, 400, 500, ___ ___ ___

8. 1,   2,   1,   3,   1,   4,   ___ ___ ___

Bonus: Design your own pattern of numerals for your class to solve.

What Is Next?

Find the pattern in each series below. Draw the next three members
of the series on the lines.

1.   11,   22,   33,   44,   ___ ___ ___

2.   1,   2,   1,   2,   1,   ___ ___ ___

3.   10,   20,   10,   20,   10,   ___ ___ ___

4.   1,   1,   2,   2,   3,   3,   ___ ___ ___

5.   1,   3,   5,   7,   9,   11,   ___ ___ ___

6.   5,   10,   15,   20,   25,   ___ ___ ___

7.   2,   4,   6,   8,   10,   ___ ___ ___

8.   1,   11,   2,   12,   3,   13,   4   ___ ___ ___

Bonus: Design your own pattern of numerals for your class to solve.

What Time Is It ?

Look at the clock below and answer the questions.

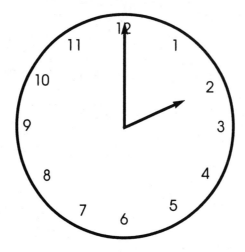

1. What time does this clock show?

_____

2. It is daylight outside. Is this time A.M or P.M.?

_____

3. What time will it be in one hour?

_____

4. What time was it one hour ago?

_____

5. Brad will eat dinner in three hours. What time will Brad eat dinner?

_____

6. The baby just woke up. He slept for two hours. What time did he go to sleep?

_____

What Time Is It ?

Look at the clock below and answer the questions.

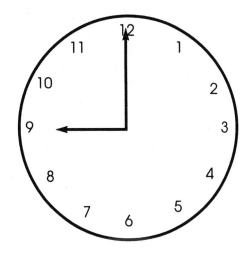

1. What time does this clock show?

_____

2. It is daylight outside. Is this time A.M or P.M.?

_____

3. What time will it be in one hour?

_____

4. What time was 2 hours ago?

_____

5. Kyle eats lunch in three hours. What time does he eat lunch?

_____

6. William woke up three hours ago. What time did William wake up?

_____

What Time Is It ?

Look at the clock below and answer the questions.

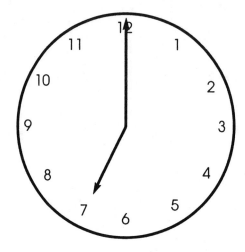

1. What time does this clock show?

_____

2. I just ate dinner. Is this time A.M or P.M.?

_____

3. What time will it be in four hours?

_____

4. What time was it two hours ago?

_____

5. Henry's bedtime is in two hours. What time does he go to bed?

_____

6. Rachel ate dinner one hour ago. What time did she eat dinner?

_____

What Time Is It ?

Look at the clock below and answer the questions.

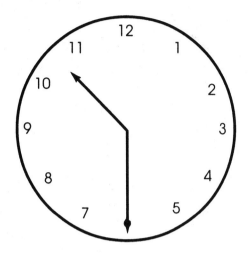

1. What time does this clock show?

_____

2. It is daylight outside. Is this time A.M or P.M.?

_____

3. What time will it be in one hour?

_____

4. What time was it one hour ago?

_____

5. Maria must read for half an hour. What time can she stop reading?

_____

6. Erna will eat in two hours. What time will she eat?

_____

What Time Is It ?

Look at the clock below and answer the questions.

1. What time does this clock show?

_____

2. It is around dinner time. Is this time A.M or P.M.?

_____

3. What time was it two hours ago?

_____

4. What time was it 30 minutes ago?

_____

5. Ryan must be home in one half hour. What time must he be home?

_____

6. Linda has been home for three hours. What time did she get home?

_____

Skills Evaluation

Choose the best answer to these review questions.
Circle the correct answer.

1. Add: 4
      +2
 	
 A. 24   B. 42
 	
 C. 6   D. 7
	2. Subtract: 5
	      - 3
	
	 A. 2 B. 3
	
	 C. 7 D. 8

3. Add: 9
      +3
 	
 A. 12   B. 13
 	
 C. 14   D. 49
	4. Subtract: 12
	      - 8
	
	 A. 20 B. 5
	
	 C. 4 D. 3

5. Subtract: 60
      - 20
 	
 A. 40   B. 50
 	
 C. 70   D. 80
	6. Add: 75
	      + 23
	
	 A. 52 B. 58
	
	 C. 92 D. 98

7. Subtract: 50
      - 10
 	
 A. 40   B. 20
 	
 C. 30   D. 60
	8. Add: 40
	      + 55
	
	 A. 95 B. 89
	
	 C. 97 D. 98

9. Subtract: 80
      - 30
 	
 A. 10   B. 50
 	
 C. 80   D. 60
	10. Add: 45
	      + 43
	
	 A. 82 B. 88
	
	 C. 62 D. 78

CD-3721

Skills Evaluation

Choose the best answer to these review questions.
Circle the correct answer.

1. Add: 3
      +1
 	
 A. 5   B. 2
 	
 C. 6   D. 4
	2. Subtract: 6
	      - 1
	
	 A. 3 B. 1
	
	 C. 5 D. 7

3. Add: 6
      +5
 	
 A. 11   B. 23
 	
 C. 13   D. 65
	4. Subtract: 10
	      - 7
	
	 A. 10 B. 5
	
	 C. 17 D. 3

5. Subtract: 35
      - 30
 	
 A. 5   B. 12
 	
 C. 65   D. 31
	6. Add: 12
	      + 8
	
	 A. 4 B. 20
	
	 C. 22 D. 90

7. Subtract: 10
      - 10
 	
 A. 0   B. 4
 	
 C. 10   D. 20
	8. Add: 23
	      +21
	
	 A. 44 B. 36
	
	 C. 45 D. 28

9. Subtract: 80
      - 30
 	
 A. 10   B. 50
 	
 C. 80   D. 60
	10. Add: 40
	      + 22
	
	 A. 22 B. 18
	
	 C. 62 D. 28

Skills Evaluation

Choose the best answer to these review questions.
Circle the correct answer.

1. Add: 9
      + 3
 	
 A. 11   B. 12
 	
 C. 4   D. 6
	2. Subtract: 9
	      - 5
	
	 A. 5 B. 14
	
	 C. 4 D. 6

3. Add: 6
      + 4
 	
 A. 14   B. 8
 	
 C. 16   D. 10
	4. Subtract: 10
	      - 6
	
	 A. 16 B. 8
	
	 C. 4 D. 5

5. Subtract: 28
      - 10
 	
 A. 3   B. 18
 	
 C. 42   D. 38
	6. Add: 75
	      + 23
	
	 A. 52 B. 58
	
	 C. 92 D. 98

7. Subtract: 10
      - 5
 	
 A. 10   B. 12
 	
 C. 15   D. 5
	8. Add: 40
	      + 35
	
	 A. 75 B. 45
	
	 C. 37 D. 5

9. Subtract: 40
      - 10
 	
 A. 40   B. 20
 	
 C. 50   D. 30
	10. Add: 25
	      + 23
	
	 A. 22 B. 48
	
	 C. 2 D. 18

Skills Evaluation

Choose the best answer to these review questions.
Circle the correct answer.

1. Add: 7
      + 2

  A. 9   B. 3

  C. 5   D. 2

2. Subtract: 8
       - 3

  A. 1   B. 12

  C. 5   D. 0

3. Add: 6
      + 4

  A. 14   B. 8

  C. 16   D. 10

4. Subtract: 15
       - 8

  A. 19   B. 11

  C. 2   D. 7

5. Subtract: 40
       - 20

  A. 60   B. 5

  C. 20   D. 14

6. Add: 75
      + 13

  A. 52   B. 58

  C. 92   D. 88

7. Subtract: 5
       - 5

  A. 0   B. 11

  C. 10   D. 6

8. Add: 30
      + 25

  A. 5   B. 55

  C. 6   D. 3

9. Subtract: 55
       - 10

  A. 45   B. 40

  C. 20   D. 65

10. Add: 15
      + 24

  A. 12   B. 39

  C. 20   D. 28

Skills Evaluation

Choose the best answer to these review questions.
Circle the correct answer.

1. Find the missing factor: $\square - 6 = 5$ A. 1 B. 2 C. 12 D. 11	**2.** Find the missing factor: $\square - 5 = 7$ A. 12 B. 11 C. 10 D. 2
3. Find the missing factor: $\square - 4 = 8$ A. 4 B. 5 C. 12 D. 11	**4.** Find the missing factor: $\square - 6 = 3$ A. 3 B. 8 C. 9 D. 10
5. Find the missing factor: $\square - 3 = 7$ A. 10 B. 11 C. 3 D. 4	**6.** Which expression does not equal 8? A. 4 + 4 B. 10 - 2 C. 11 - 4 C. 12 - 4
7. Which expression does not equal 10? A. 9 + 3 B. 10 + 0 C. 8 + 2 C. 5 + 5	**8.** Which expression does not equal 12? A. 4 + 8 B. 7 + 5 C. 3 + 8 C. 9 + 3
9. Which expression does not equal 9? A. 5 + 4 B. 10 - 1 C. 7 + 2 C. 12 - 4	**10.** Which expression does not equal 7? A. 3 + 4 B. 12 - 4 C. 9 - 2 C. 11 - 4

Skills Evaluation

Choose the best answer to these review questions.
Circle the correct answer.

1. Kelley had 12 jacks. She lost 7. How many does she have left? A. 7 B. 19 C. 6 D. 5	**2.** Meyer drove 20 miles to the store. Then he drove 20 miles back home. How many miles did he drive? A. 40 B. 20 C. 4 D. 60
3. Newton had six apples. He ate three. How many apples are left? A. 2 B. 3 C. 4 D. 9	**4.** Roger has four cats and seven dogs. How many pets does he have ? A. 10 B. 11 C. 12 D. 3
5. Alyssa had 42 stars. She gave away 21. How many are left? A. 64 B. 61 C. 23 D. 21	**6.** What number comes next? 5, 6, 7, 8, A. 4 B. 9 C. 7 D. 10
7. What number comes next? 10, 20, 30, 40, A. 45 B. 50 C. 60 D. 5	**8.** What number comes next? 15, 20, 25, 30, A. 31 B. 33 C. 35 D. 40
9. What number has a 3 in the hundreds place, 1 in the ones place, and 2 in the tens place? A. 213 B. 123 C. 321 D. 312	**10.** What number has a 9 in the tens place, 7 in the hundreds place, and 4 in the ones place? A. 794 B. 974 C. 497 D. 749

Name_____

Skills Evaluation

Choose the best answer to these review questions.
Circle the correct answer.

1. The number is 270. What number is 100 more? A. 170 B. 370 C. 270 D. 280	**2.** The number is 463. What number is 10 less? A. 363 B. 473 C. 453 D. 563
3. The number is 135. What number is 10 more? A. 235 B. 136 C. 145 D. 125	**4.** The number is 627. What number is 1 more? A. 637 B. 628 C. 727 D. 617

5. Subtract: 48
           − 36
 	
A. 72 B. 71
 	
C. 22 D. 12
	6. Subtract: 32
	           − 22
	
	A. 12 B. 10
	
	C. 54 D. 50

7. Subtract: 87
           − 53
 	
A. 34 B. 24
 	
C. 33 D. 39
	8. Subtract: 58
	           − 33
	
	A. 84 B. 26
	
	C. 25 D. 85

9. Subtract: 638
           − 224
 	
A. 454 B. 854
 	
C. 414 D. 814
	10. Subtract: 548
	           − 335
	
	A. 223 B. 213
	
	C. 813 D. 273

Name _____

Skills Evaluation

Choose the best answer to these review questions.
Circle the correct answer.

---

1. Look at the time on the clock. What time was it one hour ago?

    A. 11:00   B. 9:30   C. 11:30   D. 9:00

---

2. Look at the time on the clock. What time will it be in two more hours?

    A. 11:00   B. 3:00   C. 3:30   D. 4:00

---

3. Look at the time on the clock. What time was it one hour ago?

    A. 3:30   B. 4:00   C. 5:00   D. 5:30

---

4. Look at the time on the clock. What time was it two hours ago?

    A. 2:30   B. 6:00   C. 3:00   D. 10:30

---

5. Look at the time on the clock. What time was it one hour ago?

    A. 4:30   B. 3:00   C. 11:00   D. 10:00

---

6. Look at the time on the clock. What time will it be in one hour?

    A. 3:30   B. 4:00   C. 5:00   D. 5:30

Answer Key

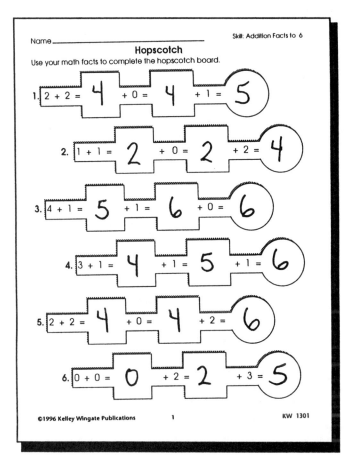

Name _____   Skill: Addition Facts to 6
Hopscotch
Use your math facts to complete the hopscotch board.

1. 2 + 2 = **4** + 0 = **4** + 1 = **5**

2. 1 + 1 = **2** + 0 = **2** + 2 = **4**

3. 4 + 1 = **5** + 1 = **6** + 0 = **6**

4. 3 + 1 = **4** + 1 = **5** + 1 = **6**

5. 2 + 2 = **4** + 0 = **4** + 2 = **6**

6. 0 + 0 = **0** + 2 = **2** + 3 = **5**

©1996 Kelley Wingate Publications   1   KW 1301

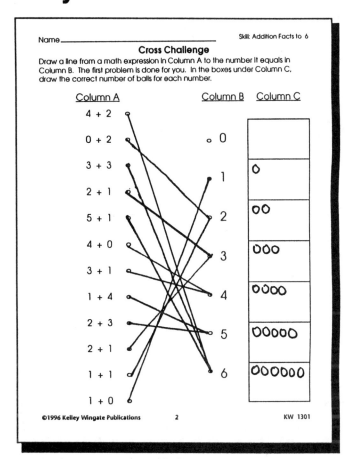

Name _____   Skill: Addition Facts to 6
Cross Challenge
Draw a line from a math expression in Column A to the number it equals in Column B. The first problem is done for you. In the boxes under Column C, draw the correct number of balls for each number.

Column A   Column B   Column C

4 + 2
0 + 2   0
3 + 3
2 + 1   1
5 + 1
4 + 0   2
3 + 1
1 + 4   3
2 + 3
2 + 1   4
1 + 1
1 + 0   5

                   6

©1996 Kelley Wingate Publications   2   KW 1301

Name _____   Skill: Addition Facts to 6
Mystery Math
Look at the mystery number. Circle all math expressions in that row which equal the mystery number. The first problem is done for you.

Mystery Number	Math Expression			
0	1 + 3	(0 + 0)	1 + 0	0 + 2
6	(1 + 5)	1 + 4	(3 + 3)	(4 + 2)
1	6 + 0	2 + 3	(1 + 0)	1 + 1
3	2 + 2	(3 + 0)	(2 + 1)	4 + 1
5	2 + 1	(4 + 1)	(3 + 2)	1 + 3
2	2 + 1	(2 + 0)	5 + 1	(1 + 1)
4	(1 + 3)	(2 + 2)	1 + 4	5 + 1

Circle all the math expressions that equal 6.

0 + 0	1 + 4	(6 + 0)	2 + 2	3 + 1
0 + 4	(5 + 1)	2 + 1	3 + 2	0 + 1
(2 + 4)	0 + 3	5 + 0	(3 + 3)	(0 + 6)

©1996 Kelley Wingate Publications   3   KW 1301

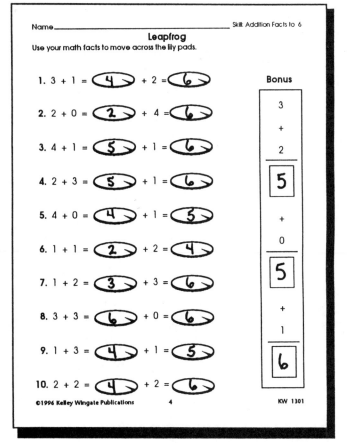

Name _____   Skill: Addition Facts to 6
Leapfrog
Use your math facts to move across the lily pads.

1. 3 + 1 = **4** + 2 = **6**

2. 2 + 0 = **2** + 4 = **6**

3. 4 + 1 = **5** + 1 = **6**

4. 2 + 3 = **5** + 1 = **6**

5. 4 + 0 = **4** + 1 = **5**

6. 1 + 1 = **2** + 2 = **4**

7. 1 + 2 = **3** + 3 = **6**

8. 3 + 3 = **6** + 0 = **6**

9. 1 + 3 = **4** + 1 = **5**

10. 2 + 2 = **4** + 2 = **6**

Bonus

3
+
2
5
+
0
5
+
1
6

©1996 Kelley Wingate Publications   4   KW 1301

Answer Key

Fact Finder

Solve each math sentence in the Facts Box. Search the puzzle for facts. Circle the whole math sentence when you find it.

FACTS BOX

0 + 2 = **2**	5 + 1 = **6**	3 + 3 = **6**
3 + 2 = **5**	2 + 4 = **6**	2 + 2 = **4**
0 + 3 = **3**	3 + 1 = **4**	1 + 4 = **5**
	0 + 6 = **6**	

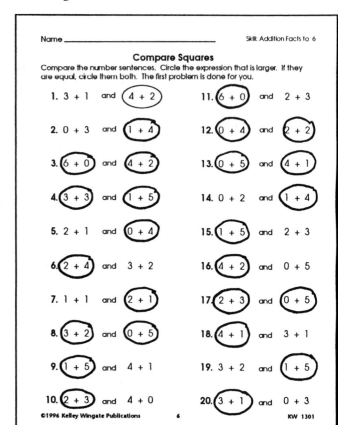

Bonus: Did you find a false math fact in the puzzle? Draw a red box around it.

Compare Squares

Compare the number sentences. Circle the expression that is larger. If they are equal, circle them both. The first problem is done for you.

1. 3 + 1   and   (4 + 2)
2. 0 + 3   and   (1 + 4)
3. (6 + 0)   and   (4 + 2)
4. (3 + 3)   and   (1 + 5)
5. 2 + 1   and   (0 + 4)
6. (2 + 4)   and   3 + 2
7. 1 + 1   and   (2 + 1)
8. (3 + 2)   and   (0 + 5)
9. (1 + 5)   and   4 + 1
10. (2 + 3)   and   4 + 0

11. (6 + 0)   and   2 + 3
12. (0 + 4)   and   (2 + 2)
13. (0 + 5)   and   (4 + 1)
14. 0 + 2   and   (1 + 4)
15. (1 + 5)   and   2 + 3
16. (4 + 2)   and   0 + 5
17. (2 + 3)   and   (0 + 5)
18. (4 + 1)   and   3 + 1
19. 3 + 2   and   (1 + 5)
20. (3 + 1)   and   0 + 3

Blankety- Blanks

Solve the problems below and write the answer in the box. On the blanket, shade in all the numbers that are in the answer boxes. The answers will make a pattern.

2 + 3 = **5**

4 + **0** = 4

3 + 3 = **6**

3 + 3 = 6

0 + **1** = 1

2 + 2 = 4

2 + **4** = 6

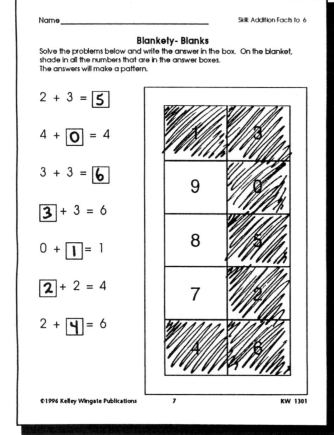

Beat the Clock

How quickly can you complete this page? Time yourself. Ready, set, go!

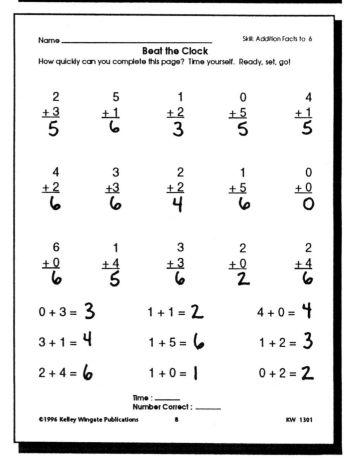

2 +3 **5**	5 +1 **6**	1 +2 **3**	0 +5 **5**	4 +1 **5**
4 +2 **6**	3 +3 **6**	2 +2 **4**	1 +5 **6**	0 +0 **0**
6 +0 **6**	1 +4 **5**	3 +3 **6**	2 +0 **2**	2 +4 **6**

0 + 3 = **3**   1 + 1 = **2**   4 + 0 = **4**

3 + 1 = **4**   1 + 5 = **6**   1 + 2 = **3**

2 + 4 = **6**   1 + 0 = **1**   0 + 2 = **2**

Time : _____
Number Correct : _____

Answer Key

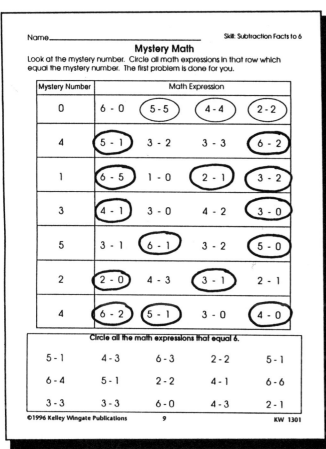

Mystery Math

Look at the mystery number. Circle all math expressions in that row which equal the mystery number. The first problem is done for you.

Mystery Number	Math Expression			
0	6 - 0	(5 - 5)	(4 - 4)	(2 - 2)
4	(5 - 1)	3 - 2	3 - 3	(6 - 2)
1	(6 - 5)	1 - 0	(2 - 1)	(3 - 2)
3	(4 - 1)	3 - 0	4 - 2	(3 - 0)
5	3 - 1	(6 - 1)	3 - 2	(5 - 0)
2	(2 - 0)	4 - 3	(3 - 1)	2 - 1
4	(6 - 2)	(5 - 1)	3 - 0	(4 - 0)

Circle all the math expressions that equal 6.				
5 - 1	4 - 3	6 - 3	2 - 2	5 - 1
6 - 4	5 - 1	2 - 2	4 - 1	6 - 6
3 - 3	3 - 3	6 - 0	4 - 3	2 - 1

©1996 Kelley Wingate Publications   9   KW 1301

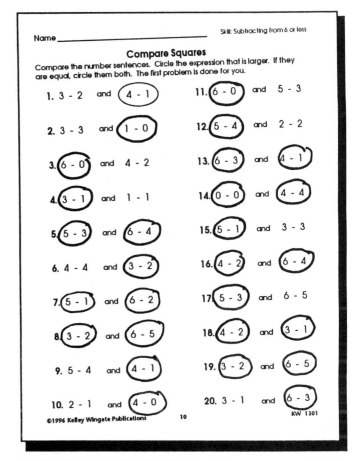

Compare Squares

Compare the number sentences. Circle the expression that is larger. If they are equal, circle them both. The first problem is done for you.

1. 3 - 2 and (4 - 1)   11. (6 - 0) and 5 - 3
2. 3 - 3 and (1 - 0)   12. (5 - 4) and 2 - 2
3. (6 - 0) and 4 - 2   13. (6 - 3) and (4 - 1)
4. (3 - 1) and 1 - 1   14. (0 - 0) and (4 - 4)
5. (5 - 3) and (6 - 4)   15. (5 - 1) and 3 - 3
6. 4 - 4 and (3 - 2)   16. (4 - 2) and (6 - 4)
7. (5 - 1) and (6 - 2)   17. (5 - 3) and 6 - 5
8. (3 - 2) and (6 - 5)   18. (4 - 2) and (3 - 1)
9. 5 - 4 and (4 - 1)   19. (3 - 2) and (6 - 5)
10. 2 - 1 and (4 - 0)   20. 3 - 1 and (6 - 3)

©1996 Kelley Wingate Publications   10   KW 1301

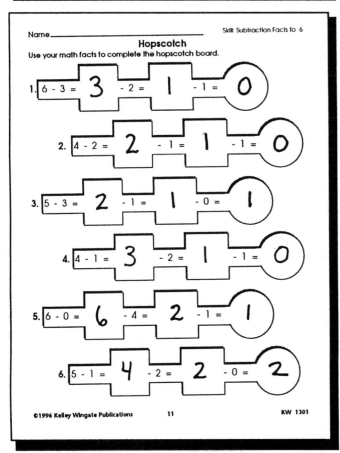

Hopscotch

Use your math facts to complete the hopscotch board.

1. 6 - 3 = **3**   - 2 = **1**   - 1 = **0**
2. 4 - 2 = **2**   - 1 = **1**   - 1 = **0**
3. 5 - 3 = **2**   - 1 = **1**   - 0 = **1**
4. 4 - 1 = **3**   - 2 = **1**   - 1 = **0**
5. 6 - 0 = **6**   - 4 = **2**   - 1 = **1**
6. 5 - 1 = **4**   - 2 = **2**   - 0 = **2**

©1996 Kelley Wingate Publications   11   KW 1301

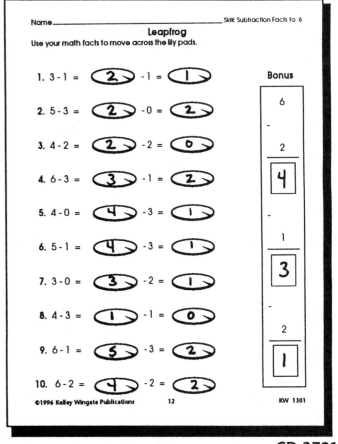

Leapfrog

Use your math facts to move across the lily pads.

1. 3 - 1 = **2**   - 1 = **1**
2. 5 - 3 = **2**   - 0 = **2**
3. 4 - 2 = **2**   - 2 = **0**
4. 6 - 3 = **3**   - 1 = **2**
5. 4 - 0 = **4**   - 3 = **1**
6. 5 - 1 = **4**   - 3 = **1**
7. 3 - 0 = **3**   - 2 = **1**
8. 4 - 3 = **1**   - 1 = **0**
9. 6 - 1 = **5**   - 3 = **2**
10. 6 - 2 = **4**   - 2 = **2**

Bonus

6
-
2
4

1
3

2
1

©1996 Kelley Wingate Publications   12   KW 1301

Answer Key

Blankety- Blanks

Solve the problems below and write the answer in the box. On the blanket, shade in all the numbers that are in the answer boxes.
The answers will make a pattern.

$3 - 3 = \boxed{0}$

$4 - \boxed{3} = 1$

$6 - 5 = \boxed{1}$

$\boxed{6} - 4 = 2$

$5 - \boxed{2} = 3$

$\boxed{5} - 4 = 1$

$6 - \boxed{4} = 2$

1	3
6	0
9	5
7	2
8	4

Fact Finder

Solve each math sentence in the Facts Box. Search the puzzle for facts.
Circle the whole math sentence when you find it.

FACTS BOX

$4 - 3 = 1$ $3 - 2 = 1$ $6 - 4 = 2$

$5 - 2 = 3$ $4 - 4 = 0$ $5 - 3 = 2$

$3 - 1 = 2$ $6 - 3 = 3$ $6 - 6 = 0$

$5 - 1 = 4$

Bonus: Did you find a false math fact in the puzzle? Draw a red box around it.

Cross Challenge

Draw a line from a math expression in Column A to the number it equals in Column B. The first problem is done for you. In the boxes under Column C, draw the correct number of balls for each number.

Column A
4 - 2
6 - 2
3 - 3
2 - 1
5 - 1
6 - 0
3 - 1
1 - 1
6 - 3
4 - 2
6 - 1
5 - 0

Column B
0
1
2
3
4
5
6

Column C

Beat the Clock

How quickly can you complete this page? Time yourself. Ready, set, go!

6 − 3 = 3	5 − 1 = 4	6 − 2 = 4	3 − 2 = 1	4 − 3 = 1
4 − 2 = 2	3 − 3 = 0	2 − 2 = 0	6 − 5 = 1	0 − 0 = 0
6 − 0 = 6	4 − 1 = 3	3 − 1 = 2	2 − 0 = 2	6 − 4 = 2

$4 - 3 = 1$ $1 - 1 = 0$ $4 - 0 = 4$

$5 - 1 = 4$ $5 - 5 = 0$ $6 - 2 = 4$

$4 - 4 = 0$ $1 - 0 = 1$ $5 - 2 = 3$

Time : _____
Number Correct : _____

Answer Key

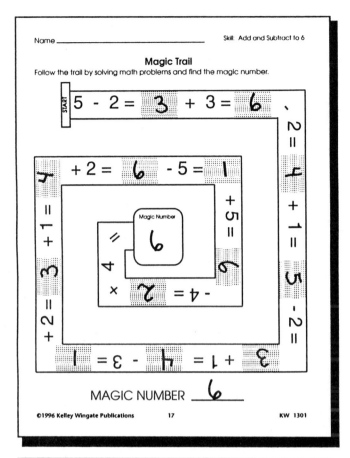

Magic Trail
Follow the trail by solving math problems and find the magic number.

START 5 - 2 = 3 + 3 = 6

+ 2 = 6   - 5 = 1

Magic Number
6

MAGIC NUMBER ___6___

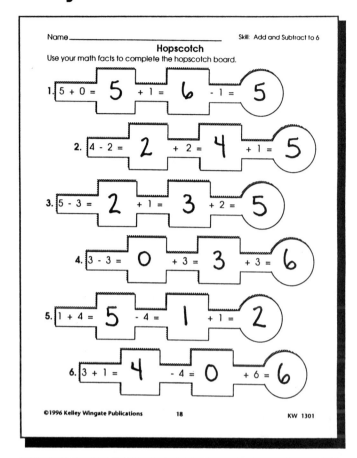

Hopscotch
Use your math facts to complete the hopscotch board.

1. 5 + 0 = 5 + 1 = 6 - 1 = 5
2. 4 - 2 = 2 + 2 = 4 + 1 = 5
3. 5 - 3 = 2 + 1 = 3 + 2 = 5
4. 3 - 3 = 0 + 3 = 3 + 3 = 6
5. 1 + 4 = 5 - 4 = 1 + 1 = 2
6. 3 + 1 = 4 - 4 = 0 + 6 = 6

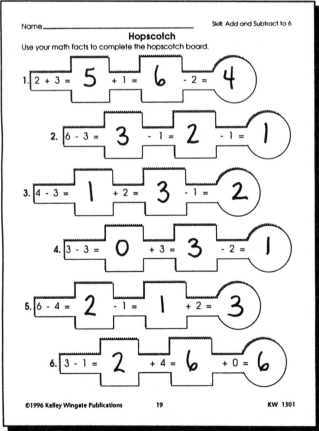

Hopscotch
Use your math facts to complete the hopscotch board.

1. 2 + 3 = 5 + 1 = 6 - 2 = 4
2. 6 - 3 = 3 - 1 = 2 - 1 = 1
3. 4 - 3 = 1 + 2 = 3 - 1 = 2
4. 3 - 3 = 0 + 3 = 3 - 2 = 1
5. 6 - 4 = 2 - 1 = 1 + 2 = 3
6. 3 - 1 = 2 + 4 = 6 + 0 = 6

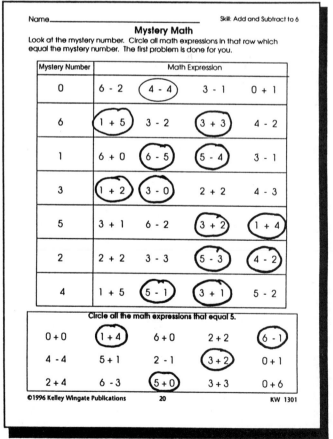

Mystery Math
Look at the mystery number. Circle all math expressions in that row which equal the mystery number. The first problem is done for you.

Mystery Number	Math Expression			
0	6 - 2	(4 - 4)	3 - 1	0 + 1
6	(1 + 5)	3 - 2	(3 + 3)	4 - 2
1	6 + 0	(6 - 5)	(5 - 4)	3 - 1
3	(1 + 2)	(3 - 0)	2 + 2	4 - 3
5	3 + 1	6 - 2	(3 + 2)	(1 + 4)
2	2 + 2	3 - 3	(5 - 3)	(4 - 2)
4	1 + 5	(5 - 1)	(3 + 1)	5 - 2

Circle all the math expressions that equal 5.

0 + 0	(1 + 4)	6 + 0	2 + 2	(6 - 1)
4 - 4	5 + 1	2 - 1	(3 + 2)	0 + 1
2 + 4	6 - 3	(5 + 0)	3 + 3	0 + 6

Answer Key

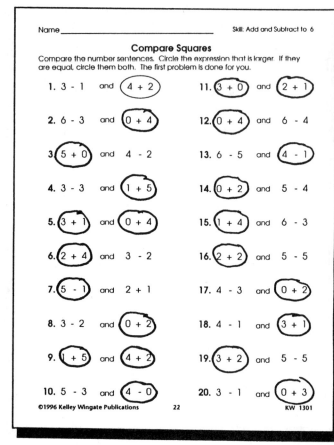

Leapfrog (top left)

Leapfrog
Use your math facts to move across the lily pads.

1. 3 + 3 = (6) - 2 = (4)
2. 6 - 3 = (3) + 2 = (5)
3. 6 - 4 = (2) - 2 = (0)
4. 1 + 3 = (4) - 2 = (2)
5. 6 - 5 = (1) + 4 = (5)
6. 2 + 4 = (6) - 3 = (3)
7. 5 - 4 = (1) + 2 = (3)
8. 5 + 0 = (5) - 1 = (4)
9. 6 - 6 = (0) + 3 = (3)
10. 5 - 2 = (3) + 1 = (4)

Bonus

4
+
2

6
-
5

1
+
3

4

Compare Squares (top right)

Compare Squares
Compare the number sentences. Circle the expression that is larger. If they are equal, circle them both. The first problem is done for you.

1. 3 - 1 and (4 + 2)
2. 6 - 3 and (0 + 4)
3. (5 + 0) and 4 - 2
4. 3 - 3 and (1 + 5)
5. (3 + 1) and (0 + 4)
6. (2 + 4) and 3 - 2
7. (5 - 1) and 2 + 1
8. 3 - 2 and (0 + 2)
9. (1 + 5) and (4 + 2)
10. 5 - 3 and (4 - 0)
11. (3 + 0) and (2 + 1)
12. (0 + 4) and 6 - 4
13. 6 - 5 and (4 - 1)
14. (0 + 2) and 5 - 4
15. (1 + 4) and 6 - 3
16. (2 + 2) and 5 - 5
17. 4 - 3 and (0 + 2)
18. 4 - 1 and (3 + 1)
19. (3 + 2) and 5 - 5
20. 3 - 1 and (0 + 3)

Family Facts Fiesta (bottom left)

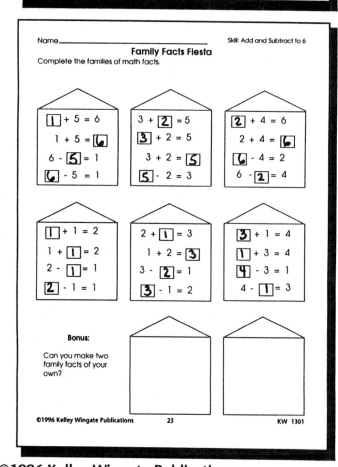

Family Facts Fiesta
Complete the families of math facts.

House 1:
[1] + 5 = 6
1 + 5 = [6]
6 - [5] = 1
[6] - 5 = 1

House 2:
3 + [2] = 5
[3] + 2 = 5
3 + 2 = [5]
[5] - 2 = 3

House 3:
[2] + 4 = 6
2 + 4 = [6]
[6] - 4 = 2
6 - [2] = 4

House 4:
[1] + 1 = 2
1 + [1] = 2
2 - [1] = 1
[2] - 1 = 1

House 5:
2 + [1] = 3
1 + 2 = [3]
3 - [2] = 1
[3] - 1 = 2

House 6:
[3] + 1 = 4
[1] + 3 = 4
[4] - 3 = 1
4 - [1] = 3

Bonus:
Can you make two family facts of your own?

Family Facts Fiesta (bottom right)

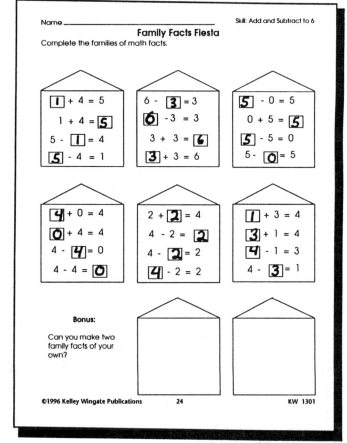

Family Facts Fiesta
Complete the families of math facts.

House 1:
[1] + 4 = 5
1 + 4 = [5]
5 - [1] = 4
[5] - 4 = 1

House 2:
6 - [3] = 3
[6] - 3 = 3
3 + 3 = [6]
[3] + 3 = 6

House 3:
[5] - 0 = 5
0 + 5 = [5]
[5] - 5 = 0
5 - [0] = 5

House 4:
[4] + 0 = 4
[0] + 4 = 4
4 - [4] = 0
4 - 4 = [0]

House 5:
2 + [2] = 4
4 - 2 = [2]
4 - [2] = 2
[4] - 2 = 2

House 6:
[1] + 3 = 4
[3] + 1 = 4
[4] - 1 = 3
4 - [3] = 1

Bonus:
Can you make two family facts of your own?

Answer Key

©1996 Kelley Wingate Publications   107   CD-3721

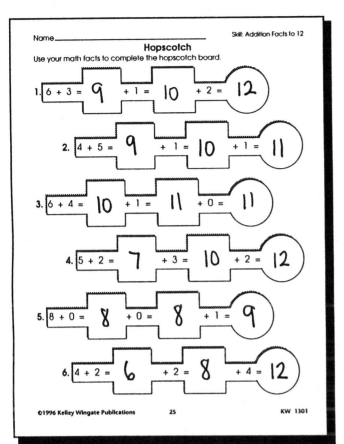

Hopscotch

Use your math facts to complete the hopscotch board.

1. 6 + 3 = 9   + 1 = 10   + 2 = 12
2. 4 + 5 = 9   + 1 = 10   + 1 = 11
3. 6 + 4 = 10   + 1 = 11   + 0 = 11
4. 5 + 2 = 7   + 3 = 10   + 2 = 12
5. 8 + 0 = 8   + 0 = 8   + 1 = 9
6. 4 + 2 = 6   + 2 = 8   + 4 = 12

©1996 Kelley Wingate Publications   25   KW 1301

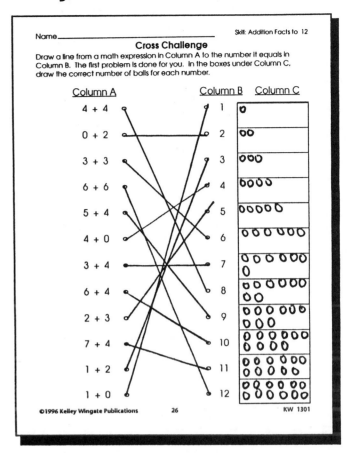

Cross Challenge

Draw a line from a math expression in Column A to the number it equals in Column B. The first problem is done for you. In the boxes under Column C, draw the correct number of balls for each number.

Column A | Column B | Column C

Column A	Column B
4 + 4	1
0 + 2	2
3 + 3	3
6 + 6	4
5 + 4	5
4 + 0	6
3 + 4	7
6 + 4	8
2 + 3	9
7 + 4	10
1 + 2	11
1 + 0	12

©1996 Kelley Wingate Publications   26   KW 1301

Mystery Math

Look at the mystery number. Circle all math expressions in that row which equal the mystery number. The first problem is done for you.

Mystery Number	Math Expression			
9	2 + 6	(6 + 3)	(4 + 5)	(1 + 8)
6	(1 + 5)	3 + 4	(3 + 3)	(4 + 2)
11	6 + 6	(8 + 3)	(7 + 4)	3 + 9
7	(5 + 2)	(3 + 4)	4 + 5	6 + 3
5	3 + 1	4 + 2	(3 + 2)	(4 + 1)
8	(4 + 4)	6 + 3	(5 + 3)	(7 + 1)
4	1 + 2	2 + 3	(3 + 1)	(2 + 2)
10	(8 + 2)	(6 + 4)	(5 + 5)	(7 + 3)
12	7 + 4	(8 + 4)	6 + 5	(9 + 3)

©1996 Kelley Wingate Publications   27   KW 1301

Leapfrog

Use your math facts to move across the lily pads.

1. 2 + 7 = (9) + 3 = (12)
2. 5 + 4 = (9) + 2 = (11)
3. 4 + 3 = (7) + 5 = (12)
4. 6 + 2 = (8) + 2 = (10)
5. 6 + 5 = (11) + 1 = (12)
6. 4 + 4 = (8) + 3 = (11)
7. 5 + 2 = (7) + 4 = (11)
8. 3 + 4 = (7) + 3 = (10)
9. 6 + 2 = (8) + 3 = (11)
10. 3 + 7 = (10) + 2 = (12)

Bonus

5
+
3

8
+
2

10
+
2

12

©1996 Kelley Wingate Publications   28   KW 1301

Answer Key

Fact Finder

Solve each math sentence in the Facts Box. Search the puzzle for facts.
Circle the whole math sentence when you find it.

FACTS BOX

$6 + 5 = 11$ $7 + 5 = 12$ $6 + 6 = 12$

$9 + 3 = 12$ $6 + 4 = 10$ $6 + 3 = 9$

$2 + 8 = 10$ $7 + 4 = 11$ $8 + 4 = 12$

$8 + 3 = 11$

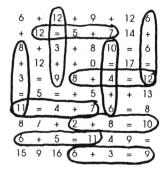

Bonus: Did you find a false math fact in the puzzle? Draw a red box around it.

©1996 Kelley Wingate Publications   29   KW 1301

Blankety- Blanks

Solve the problems below and write the answer in the box. On the blanket,
shade in all the numbers that are in the answer boxes.
The answers will make a pattern.

$8 + 4 = \boxed{12}$

$\boxed{8} + 4 = 12$

$7 + \boxed{4} = 11$

$3 + \boxed{6} = 9$

$2 + 9 = \boxed{11}$

$\boxed{7} + 3 = 10$

$\boxed{3} + 9 = 12$

$\boxed{5} + 6 = 11$

$6 + 4 = \boxed{10}$

$1 + 1 = \boxed{2}$

$\boxed{0} + 1 = 1$

$4 + 5 = \boxed{9}$

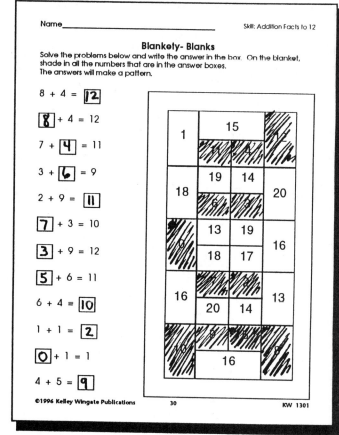

©1996 Kelley Wingate Publications   30   KW 1301

Compare Squares

Compare the number sentences. Circle the expression that is larger. If they
are equal, circle them both. The first problem is done for you.

1. $3 + 6$ and $\boxed{8 + 2}$ 11. $6 + 2$ and $\boxed{9 + 0}$

2. $\boxed{8 + 3}$ and $5 + 4$ 12. $\boxed{4 + 4}$ and $\boxed{6 + 2}$

3. $\boxed{5 + 5}$ and $\boxed{4 + 6}$ 13. $\boxed{7 + 5}$ and $6 + 4$

4. $\boxed{3 + 7}$ and $4 + 5$ 14. $8 + 2$ and $\boxed{7 + 4}$

5. $2 + 7$ and $\boxed{6 + 5}$ 15. $4 + 5$ and $\boxed{8 + 3}$

6. $\boxed{5 + 4}$ and $\boxed{3 + 6}$ 16. $1 + 6$ and $\boxed{5 + 3}$

7. $9 + 2$ and $\boxed{5 + 7}$ 17. $5 + 3$ and $\boxed{7 + 2}$

8. $3 + 6$ and $\boxed{5 + 5}$ 18. $\boxed{4 + 8}$ and $\boxed{6 + 6}$

9. $3 + 5$ and $\boxed{4 + 5}$ 19. $\boxed{7 + 3}$ and $5 + 4$

10. $2 + 7$ and $\boxed{5 + 6}$ 20. $\boxed{8 + 1}$ and $\boxed{6 + 3}$

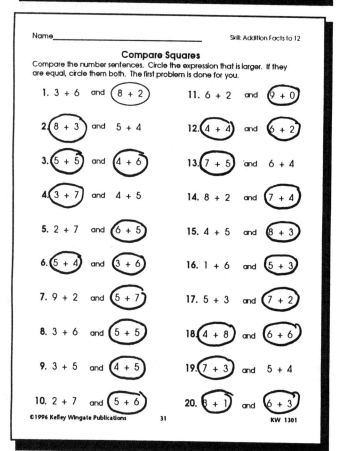

©1996 Kelley Wingate Publications   31   KW 1301

Beat the Clock

How quickly can you complete this page? Time yourself. Ready, set, go!

6	5	8	6	4
$+3$	$+5$	$+2$	$+5$	$+4$
9	10	10	11	8

6	3	9	7	8
$+4$	$+8$	$+3$	$+3$	$+1$
10	11	12	10	9

9	7	4	2	6
$+1$	$+4$	$+8$	$+9$	$+6$
10	11	12	11	12

$4 + 3 = 7$ $5 + 2 = 7$ $9 + 0 = 9$

$2 + 6 = 8$ $4 + 5 = 9$ $5 + 7 = 12$

$5 + 3 = 8$ $1 + 6 = 7$ $7 + 2 = 9$

Time : _____
Number Correct : _____

©1996 Kelley Wingate Publications   32   KW 1301

Answer Key

Blankety- Blanks

Solve the problems below and write the answer in the box. On the blanket, shade in all the numbers that are in the answer boxes.
The answers will make a pattern.

8 - 4 = [4]

[11] - 4 = 7

11 - [9] = 2

10 - [10] = 0

10 - 2 = [8]

[6] - 3 = 3

[12] - 3 = 9

[5] - 3 = 2

9 - 8 = [1]

11 - 9 = [2]

[3] - 2 = 1

10 - 3 = [7]

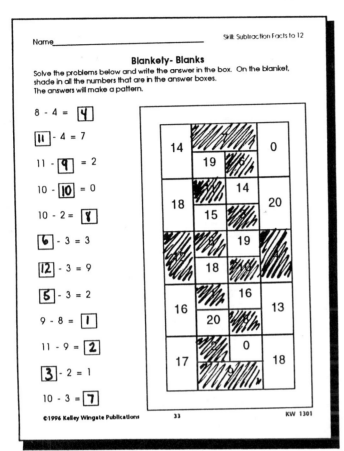

Hopscotch
Use your math facts to complete the hopscotch board.

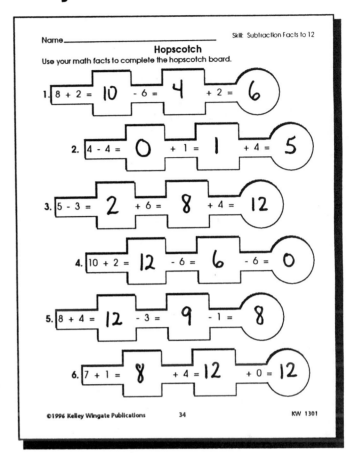

Cross Challenge
Draw a line from a math expression in Column A to the number it equals in Column B. The first problem is done for you. In the boxes under Column C, draw the correct number of X's for each number.

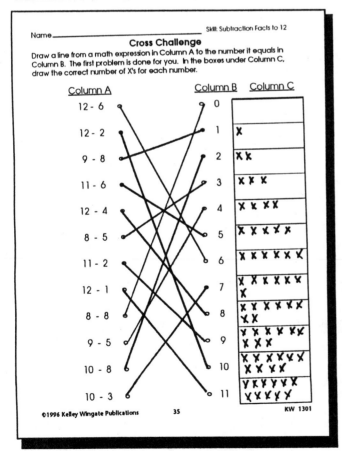

Compare Squares
Compare the number sentences. Circle the expression that is larger. If they are equal, circle them both. The first problem is done for you.

1. 12 - 8 and (9 - 2)

2. (8 - 3) and 9 - 6

3. 10 - 5 and (12 - 4)

4. (11 - 3) and 9 - 2

5. 9 - 4 and (11 - 3)

6. (12 - 4) and 9 - 3

7. (10 - 6) and (8 - 4)

8. 9 - 5 and (10 - 3)

9. 8 - 5 and (9 - 3)

10. (7 - 4) and (11 - 8)

11. (11 - 7) and 6 - 4

12. (10 - 4) and 7 - 2

13. (9 - 5) and (8 - 4)

14. (10 - 2) and (11 - 3)

15. (11 - 5) and 8 - 3

16. (9 - 3) and 10 - 5

17. (12 - 3) and 10 - 6

18. 8 - 3 and (10 - 4)

19. (11 - 8) and (9 - 6)

20. 10 - 7 and (9 - 5)

Answer Key

Mystery Math

Look at the mystery number. Circle all math expressions in that row which equal the mystery number. The first problem is done for you.

Mystery Number	Math Expression			
9	12 - 6	(12 - 3)	(10 - 1)	9 - 1
6	(11 - 5)	(10 - 4)	9 - 2	8 - 3
2	(9 - 7)	8 - 5	(11 - 9)	7 - 3
7	11 - 5	10 - 4	(12 - 5)	(9 - 2)
5	(10 - 5)	(9 - 4)	11 - 7	12 - 8
8	9 - 2	10 - 3	(11 - 3)	(12 - 4)
4	(8 - 4)	10 - 7	(9 - 5)	11 - 6
1	10 - 8	(8 - 7)	6 - 2	(7 - 6)
3	(10 - 7)	(12 - 9)	(9 - 6)	11 - 7

©1996 Kelley Wingate Publications   37   KW 1301

Leapfrog

Use your math facts to move across the lily pads.

1. 12 - 5 = (7) - 6 = (1)
2. 11 - 9 = (2) - 1 = (1)
3. 10 - 3 = (7) - 4 = (3)
4. 9 - 5 = (4) - 2 = (2)
5. 11 - 2 = (9) - 4 = (5)
6. 12 - 3 = (9) - 3 = (6)
7. 11 - 7 = (4) - 2 = (2)
8. 10 - 5 = (5) - 4 = (1)
9. 9 - 2 = (7) - 2 = (5)
10. 12 - 4 = (8) - 5 = (3)

Bonus

$$\begin{array}{r} 11 \\ - 5 \\ \hline 6 \\ - 4 \\ \hline 2 \\ - 2 \\ \hline 0 \end{array}$$

©1996 Kelley Wingate Publications   38   KW 1301

Blankety- Blanks

Solve the problems below and write the answer in the box. On the blanket, shade in all the numbers that are in the answer boxes. The answers will make a pattern.

9 - 3 = [6]

[12] - 6 = 6

10 - [8] = 2

12 - [9] = 3

10 - 6 = [4]

[3] - 2 = 1

[11] - 3 = 8

[10] - 5 = 5

9 - 7 = [2]

11 - 4 = [7]

[5] - 2 = 3

10 - 9 = [1]

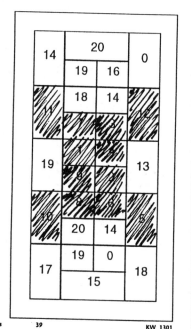

©1996 Kelley Wingate Publications   39   KW 1301

Beat the Clock

How quickly can you complete this page? Time yourself. Ready, set, go!

$\begin{array}{r}8\\-3\\\hline 5\end{array}$	$\begin{array}{r}9\\-4\\\hline 5\end{array}$	$\begin{array}{r}10\\-5\\\hline 5\end{array}$	$\begin{array}{r}11\\-3\\\hline 8\end{array}$	$\begin{array}{r}7\\-4\\\hline 3\end{array}$
$\begin{array}{r}12\\-9\\\hline 3\end{array}$	$\begin{array}{r}10\\-6\\\hline 4\end{array}$	$\begin{array}{r}12\\-3\\\hline 9\end{array}$	$\begin{array}{r}11\\-5\\\hline 6\end{array}$	$\begin{array}{r}10\\-8\\\hline 2\end{array}$
$\begin{array}{r}11\\-7\\\hline 4\end{array}$	$\begin{array}{r}10\\-4\\\hline 6\end{array}$	$\begin{array}{r}9\\-5\\\hline 4\end{array}$	$\begin{array}{r}11\\-6\\\hline 5\end{array}$	$\begin{array}{r}12\\-7\\\hline 5\end{array}$

9 - 6 = 3   11 - 8 = 3   8 - 5 = 3

10 - 7 = 3   12 - 6 = 6   11 - 4 = 7

12 - 5 = 7   10 - 2 = 8   11 - 9 = 2

Time : _____
Number Correct : _____

©1996 Kelley Wingate Publications   40   KW 1301

Answer Key

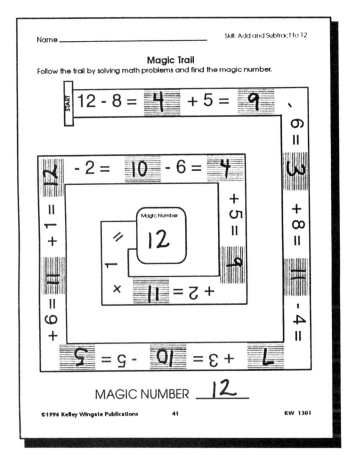

Name_____ Skill: Add and Subtract to 12

Magic Trail
Follow the trail by solving math problems and find the magic number.

START 12 - 8 = 4 + 5 = 9

-2 = 10 - 6 = 4

Magic Number 12

MAGIC NUMBER 12

©1996 Kelley Wingate Publications   41   KW 1301

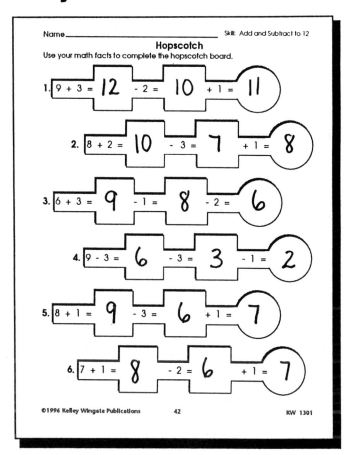

Name_____ Skill: Add and Subtract to 12

Hopscotch
Use your math facts to complete the hopscotch board.

1. 9 + 3 = 12 - 2 = 10 + 1 = 11
2. 8 + 2 = 10 - 3 = 7 + 1 = 8
3. 6 + 3 = 9 - 1 = 8 - 2 = 6
4. 9 - 3 = 6 - 3 = 3 - 1 = 2
5. 8 + 1 = 9 - 3 = 6 + 1 = 7
6. 7 + 1 = 8 - 2 = 6 + 1 = 7

©1996 Kelley Wingate Publications   42   KW 1301

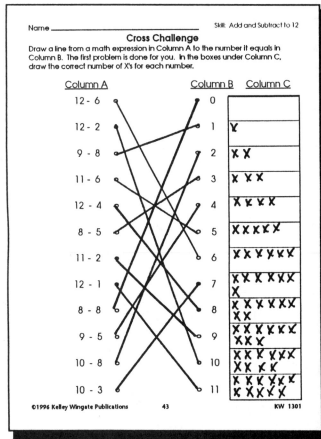

Name_____ Skill: Add and Subtract to 12

Cross Challenge
Draw a line from a math expression in Column A to the number it equals in Column B. The first problem is done for you. In the boxes under Column C, draw the correct number of X's for each number.

Column A   Column B   Column C

12 - 6	0	
12 - 2	1	X
9 - 8	2	X X
11 - 6	3	X X X
12 - 4	4	X X X X
8 - 5	5	X X X X X
11 - 2	6	X X X X X X
12 - 1	7	X X X X X X X
8 - 8	8	X X X X X X X X
9 - 5	9	X X X X X X X X X
10 - 8	10	X X X X X X X X X X
10 - 3	11	X X X X X X X X X X X

©1996 Kelley Wingate Publications   43   KW 1301

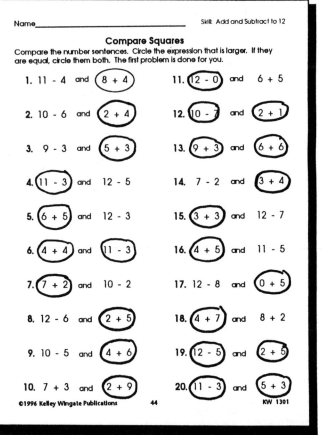

Name_____ Skill: Add and Subtract to 12

Compare Squares
Compare the number sentences. Circle the expression that is larger. If they are equal, circle them both. The first problem is done for you.

1. 11 - 4 and (8 + 4)
2. 10 - 6 and (2 + 4)
3. 9 - 3 and (5 + 3)
4. (11 - 3) and 12 - 5
5. (6 + 5) and 12 - 3
6. (4 + 4) and (11 - 3)
7. (7 + 2) and 10 - 2
8. 12 - 6 and (2 + 5)
9. 10 - 5 and (4 + 6)
10. 7 + 3 and (2 + 9)

11. (12 - 0) and 6 + 5
12. (10 - 7) and (2 + 1)
13. (9 + 3) and (6 + 6)
14. 7 - 2 and (3 + 4)
15. (3 + 3) and 12 - 7
16. (4 + 5) and 11 - 5
17. 12 - 8 and (0 + 5)
18. (4 + 7) and 8 + 2
19. (12 - 5) and (2 + 5)
20. (11 - 3) and (5 + 3)

©1996 Kelley Wingate Publications   44   KW 1301

Answer Key

Name _____   Skill: Add and Subtract to 12

Blankety- Blanks

Solve the problems below and write the answer in the box. On the blanket, shade in all the numbers that are in the answer boxes.
The answers will make a pattern.

9 + 3 = $\boxed{12}$

$\boxed{7}$ - 6 = 1

10 - $\boxed{1}$ = 9

3 + $\boxed{8}$ = 11

10 - 4 = $\boxed{6}$

$\boxed{11}$ - 6 = 5

$\boxed{4}$ + 3 = 7

$\boxed{3}$ + 7 = 10

12 - 7 = $\boxed{5}$

8 + 2 = $\boxed{10}$

$\boxed{9}$ - 2 = 7

6 - 4 = $\boxed{2}$

19	16
18	14
17	13
0	14
19	20
18	16
20	14
19	0

©1996 Kelley Wingate Publications   45   KW 1301

Name _____   Skill: Add and Subtract to 12

Family Facts Fiesta
Complete the families of math facts.

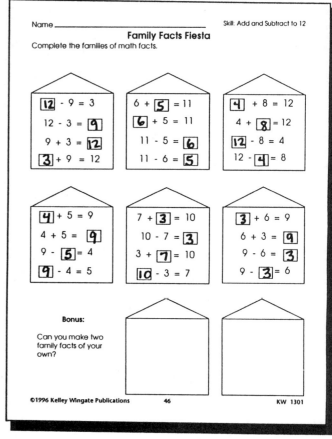

$\boxed{12}$ - 9 = 3
12 - 3 = $\boxed{9}$
9 + 3 = $\boxed{12}$
$\boxed{3}$ + 9 = 12

6 + $\boxed{5}$ = 11
$\boxed{6}$ + 5 = 11
11 - 5 = $\boxed{6}$
11 - 6 = $\boxed{5}$

$\boxed{4}$ + 8 = 12
4 + $\boxed{8}$ = 12
$\boxed{12}$ - 8 = 4
12 - $\boxed{4}$ = 8

$\boxed{4}$ + 5 = 9
4 + 5 = $\boxed{9}$
9 - $\boxed{5}$ = 4
$\boxed{9}$ - 4 = 5

7 + $\boxed{3}$ = 10
10 - 7 = $\boxed{3}$
3 + $\boxed{7}$ = 10
$\boxed{10}$ - 3 = 7

$\boxed{3}$ + 6 = 9
6 + 3 = $\boxed{9}$
9 - 6 = $\boxed{3}$
9 - $\boxed{3}$ = 6

Bonus:

Can you make two family facts of your own?

©1996 Kelley Wingate Publications   46   KW 1301

Name _____   Skill: Add and Subtract to 12

Family Facts Fiesta
Complete the families of math facts.

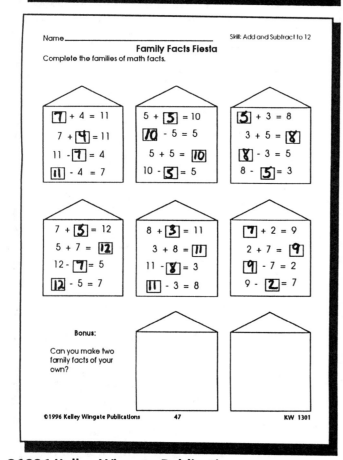

$\boxed{7}$ + 4 = 11
7 + $\boxed{4}$ = 11
11 - $\boxed{7}$ = 4
$\boxed{11}$ - 4 = 7

5 + $\boxed{5}$ = 10
$\boxed{10}$ - 5 = 5
5 + 5 = $\boxed{10}$
10 - $\boxed{5}$ = 5

$\boxed{5}$ + 3 = 8
3 + 5 = $\boxed{8}$
$\boxed{8}$ - 3 = 5
8 - $\boxed{5}$ = 3

7 + $\boxed{5}$ = 12
5 + 7 = $\boxed{12}$
12 - $\boxed{7}$ = 5
$\boxed{12}$ - 5 = 7

8 + $\boxed{3}$ = 11
3 + 8 = $\boxed{11}$
11 - $\boxed{8}$ = 3
$\boxed{11}$ - 3 = 8

$\boxed{7}$ + 2 = 9
2 + 7 = $\boxed{9}$
$\boxed{9}$ - 7 = 2
9 - $\boxed{2}$ = 7

Bonus:

Can you make two family facts of your own?

©1996 Kelley Wingate Publications   47   KW 1301

Name _____   Skill: Place Value to Hundreds

I' m thinking of a number....
Read the clues and write the numbers in the proper place on the grid.

1. I'm thinking of a number with a 3 in the hundreds place, a 2 in the ones place, and a 4 in the tens place.
What is the number?

$\underset{H}{3} \quad \underset{T}{4} \quad \underset{O}{2}$

2. I'm thinking of a number with a 6 in the ones place, a 2 in the the tens place and a 7 in the hundreds place.
What is the number?

$\underset{H}{7} \quad \underset{T}{2} \quad \underset{O}{6}$

3. I'm thinking of a number with a 2 in the ones place, an 8 in the tens place, and a 3 in the hundreds place.
What is the number?

$\underset{H}{3} \quad \underset{T}{8} \quad \underset{O}{2}$

4. I'm thinking of a number with a 9 in the tens place, a 4 in the ones place, and a 1 in the hundreds place.
What is the number?

$\underset{H}{1} \quad \underset{T}{9} \quad \underset{O}{4}$

5. I'm thinking of a number with a 5 in the tens place, a 2 in the hundreds place, and a 7 in the ones place.
What is the number?

$\underset{H}{2} \quad \underset{T}{5} \quad \underset{O}{7}$

©1996 Kelley Wingate Publications   48   KW 1301

Answer Key

I'm thinking of a number....
Read the clues and write the numbers in the proper place on the grid.

1. I'm thinking of a number with a 5 in the ones place, a 1 in the tens place, and a 3 in the hundreds place. What is the number?

$$\underset{H}{3} \quad \underset{T}{1} \quad \underset{O}{5}$$

2. I'm thinking of a number with an 8 in the tens place, a 4 in the hundreds place, and a 9 in the ones place. What is the number?

$$\underset{H}{4} \quad \underset{T}{8} \quad \underset{O}{9}$$

3. I'm thinking of a number with a 2 in the tens place, a 6 in the hundreds place, and a 4 in the ones place. What is the number?

$$\underset{H}{6} \quad \underset{T}{2} \quad \underset{O}{4}$$

4. I'm thinking of a number with a 3 in the ones place, a 2 in the tens place, and a 7 in the hundreds place. What is the number?

$$\underset{H}{7} \quad \underset{T}{2} \quad \underset{O}{3}$$

5. I'm thinking of a number with a 3 in the ones and tens places, and a 6 in the hundreds place. What is the number?

$$\underset{H}{6} \quad \underset{T}{3} \quad \underset{O}{3}$$

©1996 Kelley Wingate Publications   49   KW 1301

Which Digit?
Read the problems carefully. Answer the questions.

1. The number is **423**.

   A. Which digit is in the hundreds place? __4__
   B. Which digit is in the tens place? __2__
   C. Which digit is in the ones place? __3__

2. The number is **201**.

   A. Which digit is in the tens place? __0__
   B. Which digit is in the hundreds place? __2__
   C. Which digit is in the ones place? __1__

3. The number is **126**.

   A. Which digit is in the tens place? __2__
   B. Which digit is in the hundreds place? __1__
   C. Which digit is in the ones place? __6__

4. The number is **314**.

   A. Which digit is in the ones place? __4__
   B. Which digit is in the hundreds place? __3__
   C. Which digit is in the tens? __1__

4. The number is **541**.

   A. Which digit is in the ones place? __1__
   B. Which digit is in the hundreds place? __5__
   C. Which digit is in the tens? __4__

©1996 Kelley Wingate Publications   50   KW 1301

Place Value Polka
Read the problems carefully then name the new numbers.

1. The number is **114**.

   A. Name the number that is 10 more. __124__
   B. Name the number that is 100 less. __14__
   C. Name the number that is 10 less. __104__
   D. Name the number that is 1 more. __115__

2. The number is **356**.

   A. Name the number that is 1 less. __355__
   B. Name the number that is 100 more. __456__
   C. Name the number that is 10 less. __346__
   D. Name the number that is 10 more. __366__

3. The number is **473**.

   A. Name the number that is 10 less. __463__
   B. Name the number that is 100 less. __373__
   C. Name the number that is 100 more. __573__
   D. Name the number that is 1 more. __474__

4. The number is **225**.

   A. Name the number that is 10 more. __235__
   B. Name the number that is 100 less. __125__
   C. Name the number that is 1 less. __224__
   D. Name the number that is 10 less. __215__

©1996 Kelley Wingate Publications   51   KW 1301

Place Value Polka
Read the problems carefully then name the new numbers.

1. The number is **678**.

   A. Name the number that is 100 less. __578__
   B. Name the number that is 100 more. __778__
   C. Name the number that is 10 more. __688__
   D. Name the number that is 10 less. __668__

2. The number is **306**.

   A. Name the number that is 100 more. __406__
   B. Name the number that is 100 less. __206__
   C. Name the number that is 10 more. __316__
   D. Name the number that is 1 more. __307__

3. The number is **421**.

   A. Name the number that is 1 less. __420__
   B. Name the number that is 10 more. __431__
   C. Name the number that is 100 less. __321__
   D. Name the number that is 100 more. __521__

4. The number is **294**.

   A. Name the number that is 100 more. __394__
   B. Name the number that is 100 less. __194__
   C. Name the number that is 10 less. __284__
   D. Name the number that is 1 more. __295__

©1996 Kelley Wingate Publications   52   KW 1301

Answer Key

Compare Squares

Compare the number sentences. Circle the expression that is larger. If they are equal, circle them both. The first problem is done for you.

1. 600 and (700)
2. 200 and (300)
3. 500 and (600)
4. (800) and 700
5. 100 and (200)
6. (800) and 600
7. (900) and 600
8. 300 and (400)
9. (200) and (200)
10. 400 and (500)

11. 199 and (200)
12. (400) and 395
13. (305) and 295
14. (615) and 590
15. 125 and (210)
16. 460 and (520)
17. (825) and 725
18. (450) and 430
19. (575) and 560
20. 355 and (375)

Compare Squares

Compare the number sentences. Circle the expression that is larger. If they are equal, circle them both. The first problem is done for you.

1. 456 and (465)
2. 219 and (291)
3. 117 and (711)
4. (531) and 351
5. (222) and 221
6. (405) and 399
7. 638 and (683)
8. 109 and (110)
9. 274 and (472)
10. 689 and (986)

11. 413 and (431)
12. (770) and 707
13. (564) and 546
14. (988) and (988)
15. 315 and (331)
16. (664) and 464
17. 235 and (325)
18. 115 and (151)
19. (234) and 156
20. 133 and (313)

Adding Two-Digit Numbers

30 + 20 **50**	70 + 10 **80**	20 + 50 **70**	70 + 20 **90**	40 + 30 **70**
50 + 20 **70**	30 + 40 **70**	20 + 70 **90**	60 + 10 **70**	50 + 40 **90**
61 + 30 **91**	43 + 40 **83**	86 + 10 **96**	24 + 60 **84**	74 + 10 **84**
77 + 20 **97**	23 + 30 **53**	36 + 30 **66**	63 + 20 **83**	21 + 40 **61**

10 + 10 = **20**   20 + 20 = **40**   30 + 40 = **70**   50 + 40 = **90**

16 + 30 = **46**   50 + 11 = **61**   48 + 20 = **68**   70 + 14 = **84**

31 + 18 = **49**   22 + 44 = **66**   75 + 14 = **89**   43 + 33 = **76**

Adding Two-Digit Numbers

30 + 20 **50**	40 + 30 **70**	20 + 40 **60**	70 + 20 **90**	70 + 10 **80**
50 + 20 **70**	50 + 40 **90**	20 + 30 **50**	60 + 10 **70**	30 + 40 **70**
61 + 30 **91**	74 + 10 **84**	86 + 10 **96**	24 + 60 **84**	43 + 40 **83**
77 + 20 **97**	21 + 40 **61**	36 + 30 **66**	63 + 20 **83**	23 + 30 **53**

35 + 20 = **55**   64 + 21 = **85**   33 + 54 = **87**   12 + 24 = **36**

10 + 22 = **32**   30 + 17 = **47**   28 + 30 = **58**   42 + 35 = **77**

41 + 12 = **53**   23 + 40 = **63**   45 + 22 = **67**   15 + 12 = **27**

Answer Key

Worksheet 1

Name _____ Skill: Addition of 2 Digit Numbers

Adding Two-Digit Numbers

27 + 41 = 68	25 + 30 = 55	66 + 22 = 88	42 + 37 = 79	40 + 35 = 75
50 + 39 = 89	24 + 54 = 78	15 + 43 = 58	42 + 33 = 75	53 + 21 = 74
50 + 36 = 86	41 + 28 = 69	23 + 46 = 69	17 + 40 = 57	76 + 22 = 98
70 + 16 = 86	36 + 23 = 59	36 + 30 = 66	54 + 32 = 86	15 + 14 = 29

30 + 23 = 53   47 + 21 = 68   22 + 54 = 76   80 + 12 = 92

13 + 64 = 77   24 + 61 = 85   30 + 55 = 85   55 + 14 = 69

43 + 15 = 58   42 + 27 = 69   21 + 20 = 41   14 + 51 = 65

Worksheet 2

Name _____ Skill: Addition of 3 Digit Numbers

Adding 3 Digit Numbers

300 + 400 = 700	400 + 100 = 500	300 + 200 = 500	700 + 100 = 800	500 + 300 = 800
500 + 100 = 600	300 + 600 = 900	200 + 400 = 600	800 + 100 = 900	200 + 200 = 400
550 + 230 = 780	420 + 460 = 880	560 + 320 = 880	280 + 410 = 690	170 + 520 = 690
585 + 110 = 695	132 + 163 = 295	347 + 131 = 478	397 + 202 = 599	723 + 223 = 946

200 + 590 = 790   250 + 300 = 550   470 + 100 = 570

530 + 250 = 780   350 + 409 = 759   240 + 445 = 685

518 + 270 = 788   277 + 111 = 388   363 + 125 = 488

Worksheet 3

Name _____ Skill: Addition of 3 Digit Numbers

Adding 3 Digit Numbers

200 + 100 = 300	500 + 200 = 700	600 + 300 = 900	300 + 400 = 700	200 + 100 = 300
400 + 300 = 700	200 + 400 = 600	300 + 500 = 800	200 + 500 = 700	100 + 100 = 200
420 + 220 = 640	520 + 320 = 840	620 + 230 = 850	456 + 312 = 768	350 + 320 = 670
505 + 310 = 815	242 + 253 = 495	525 + 132 = 657	406 + 321 = 727	625 + 333 = 958

300 + 450 = 750   540 + 355 = 895   350 + 220 = 570

230 + 330 = 560   650 + 341 = 991   225 + 311 = 536

418 + 230 = 648   127 + 451 = 578   320 + 355 = 675

Worksheet 4

Name _____ Skill: Addition of 3 Digit Numbers

Adding 3 Digit Numbers

326 + 322 = 648	132 + 231 = 363	438 + 250 = 688	345 + 220 = 565	407 + 131 = 538
574 + 222 = 796	534 + 400 = 934	325 + 460 = 785	561 + 312 = 873	525 + 272 = 797
602 + 233 = 835	240 + 439 = 679	582 + 115 = 697	140 + 140 = 280	626 + 133 = 759
770 + 105 = 875	123 + 643 = 766	376 + 313 = 689	631 + 257 = 888	813 + 142 = 955

260 + 103 = 363   421 + 255 = 676   340 + 401 = 741

435 + 122 = 557   533 + 130 = 663   455 + 244 = 699

615 + 132 = 747   327 + 221 = 548   306 + 103 = 409

Answer Key

Worksheet 1 (page 61)

Name _____ Skill: Subtraction of 2 Digit Numbers

Subtracting 2 Digit Numbers

30 − 20 = 10	70 − 10 = 60	80 − 50 = 30	70 − 30 = 40	40 − 30 = 10
50 − 40 = 10	40 − 20 = 20	60 − 50 = 10	60 − 10 = 50	50 − 20 = 30
69 − 30 = 39	55 − 30 = 25	83 − 10 = 73	92 − 50 = 42	78 − 10 = 68
78 − 10 = 68	99 − 20 = 79	88 − 20 = 68	65 − 20 = 45	86 − 40 = 46

20 - 10 = 10   40 - 20 = 20   80 - 40 = 40   70 - 40 = 30

86 - 30 = 56   55 - 10 = 45   68 - 10 = 58   71 - 30 = 41

34 - 10 = 24   67 - 40 = 27   77 - 10 = 67   49 - 30 = 19

©1996 Kelley Wingate Publications   61   KW 1301

Worksheet 2 (page 62)

Name _____ Skill: Subtraction of 2 Digit Numbers

Subtracting 2 Digit Numbers

98 − 27 = 71	66 − 43 = 23	89 − 38 = 51	78 − 37 = 41	43 − 21 = 22
75 − 54 = 21	94 − 23 = 71	68 − 36 = 32	68 − 12 = 56	54 − 31 = 23
84 − 22 = 62	27 − 15 = 12	78 − 45 = 33	95 − 54 = 41	76 − 15 = 61
76 − 43 = 33	96 − 76 = 20	88 − 57 = 31	48 − 23 = 25	69 − 44 = 25

49 - 27 = 22   59 - 25 = 34   87 - 37 = 50   65 - 13 = 52

81 - 41 = 40   57 - 34 = 23   62 - 11 = 51   77 - 34 = 43

37 - 21 = 16   68 - 32 = 36   79 - 53 = 26   43 - 21 = 22

©1996 Kelley Wingate Publications   62   KW 1301

Worksheet 3 (page 63)

Name _____ Skill: Subtraction of 2 Digit Numbers

Subtracting 2 Digit Numbers

65 − 32 = 33	76 − 53 = 23	99 − 33 = 66	52 − 41 = 11	66 − 42 = 24
55 − 21 = 34	98 − 31 = 67	45 − 23 = 22	68 − 21 = 47	65 − 44 = 21
99 − 35 = 64	78 − 12 = 66	59 − 45 = 14	84 − 24 = 60	87 − 25 = 62
56 − 23 = 33	35 − 21 = 14	79 − 42 = 37	58 − 41 = 17	74 − 21 = 53

48 - 26 = 22   58 - 35 = 23   67 - 36 = 31   74 - 10 = 64

71 - 40 = 31   55 - 33 = 22   52 - 12 = 40   78 - 33 = 45

67 - 23 = 44   78 - 52 = 26   69 - 43 = 26   33 - 22 = 11

©1996 Kelley Wingate Publications   63   KW 1301

Worksheet 4 (page 64)

Name _____ Skill: Subtraction of 2 Digit Numbers

Subtracting 2 Digit Numbers

68 − 51 = 17	63 − 63 = 0	91 − 30 = 61	88 − 36 = 52	42 − 31 = 11
54 − 21 = 33	54 − 13 = 41	79 − 30 = 49	98 − 32 = 66	44 − 33 = 11
46 − 12 = 34	48 − 13 = 35	65 − 22 = 43	45 − 24 = 21	56 − 14 = 42
87 − 65 = 22	78 − 45 = 33	45 − 14 = 31	21 − 11 = 10	60 − 40 = 20

59 - 31 = 28   66 - 35 = 31   94 - 33 = 61   78 - 15 = 63

71 - 21 = 50   77 - 64 = 13   65 - 21 = 44   87 - 32 = 55

57 - 31 = 26   88 - 52 = 36   71 - 50 = 21   53 - 22 = 31

©1996 Kelley Wingate Publications   64   KW 1301

Answer Key

Subtracting 3 Digit Numbers

250	500	300	800	600
- 100	- 400	- 100	- 500	- 300
150	**100**	**200**	**300**	**300**

700	800	500	700	500
- 400	- 100	- 200	- 400	- 400
300	**700**	**300**	**300**	**100**

550	760	680	670	560
- 350	- 530	- 270	- 340	- 120
200	**230**	**410**	**330**	**440**

680	340	560	530	980
- 270	- 220	- 430	- 310	- 710
410	**120**	**130**	**220**	**270**

300 - 200 = **100**   480 - 320 = **160**   800 - 400 = **400**

650 - 130 = **520**   670 - 470 = **200**   570 - 340 = **230**

790 - 160 = **630**   380 - 150 = **230**   650 - 340 = **310**

Subtracting 3 Digit Numbers

500	800	850	440	300
- 100	- 700	- 330	- 120	- 200
400	**100**	**520**	**320**	**100**

600	400	650	620	500
- 400	- 200	- 420	- 200	- 400
200	**200**	**230**	**420**	**100**

570	580	870	505	410
- 330	- 260	- 250	- 105	- 310
240	**320**	**620**	**400**	**100**

650	370	360	790	450
- 320	- 250	- 210	- 320	- 230
330	**120**	**150**	**470**	**220**

400 - 300 = **100**   320 - 110 = **210**   650 - 420 = **230**

650 - 150 = **500**   250 - 130 = **120**   430 - 320 = **110**

670 - 160 = **510**   460 - 130 = **330**   540 - 340 = **200**

Subtracting 3 Digit Numbers

300	900	400	300	400
- 200	- 600	- 200	- 100	- 100
100	**300**	**200**	**200**	**300**

800	600	800	500	700
- 500	- 400	- 400	- 300	- 200
300	**200**	**400**	**200**	**500**

630	640	590	250	480
- 230	- 430	- 180	- 140	- 110
400	**210**	**410**	**110**	**370**

780	420	490	630	810
- 170	- 110	- 330	- 220	- 610
610	**310**	**160**	**410**	**200**

200 - 100 = **100**   400 - 200 = **200**   800 - 700 = **100**

430 - 120 = **310**   580 - 180 = **400**   490 - 240 = **250**

680 - 170 = **510**   360 - 120 = **240**   340 - 140 = **200**

Subtracting 3 Digit Numbers

826	973	843	688	537
- 610	- 650	- 720	- 370	- 430
216	**323**	**123**	**318**	**107**

729	694	875	459	767
- 412	- 453	- 462	- 249	- 253
317	**241**	**413**	**210**	**514**

888	674	564	297	899
- 526	- 341	- 221	- 186	- 487
362	**333**	**343**	**111**	**412**

365	558	846	648	866
- 163	- 223	- 305	- 238	- 242
202	**335**	**541**	**410**	**624**

642 - 330 = **312**   796 - 590 = **206**   843 - 740 = **103**

457 - 236 = **221**   659 - 324 = **335**   485 - 321 = **164**

978 - 267 = **711**   897 - 433 = **464**   774 - 573 = **201**

Answer Key

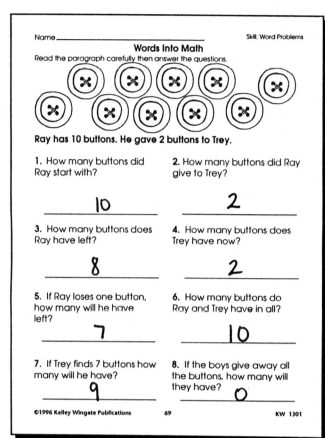

Name _____ Skill: Word Problems
Words Into Math
Read the paragraph carefully then answer the questions.

Ray has 10 buttons. He gave 2 buttons to Trey.

1. How many buttons did Ray start with?

10

2. How many buttons did Ray give to Trey?

2

3. How many buttons does Ray have left?

8

4. How many buttons does Trey have now?

2

5. If Ray loses one button, how many will he have left?

7

6. How many buttons do Ray and Trey have in all?

10

7. If Trey finds 7 buttons how many will he have?

9

8. If the boys give away all the buttons, how many will they have?

0

©1996 Kelley Wingate Publications   69   KW 1301

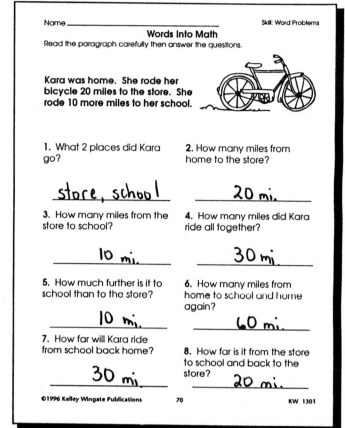

Name _____ Skill: Word Problems
Words Into Math
Read the paragraph carefully then answer the questions.

Kara was home. She rode her bicycle 20 miles to the store. She rode 10 more miles to her school.

1. What 2 places did Kara go?

store, school

2. How many miles from home to the store?

20 mi.

3. How many miles from the store to school?

10 mi.

4. How many miles did Kara ride all together?

30 mi.

5. How much further is it to school than to the store?

10 mi.

6. How many miles from home to school and home again?

60 mi.

7. How far will Kara ride from school back home?

30 mi.

8. How far is it from the store to school and back to the store?

20 mi.

©1996 Kelley Wingate Publications   70   KW 1301

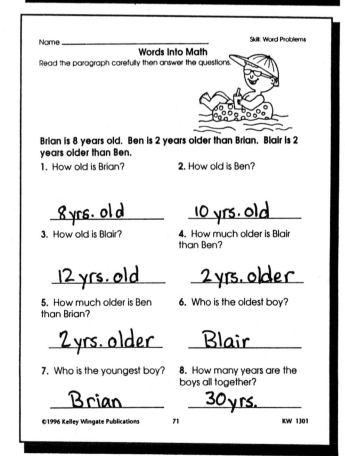

Name _____ Skill: Word Problems
Words Into Math
Read the paragraph carefully then answer the questions.

Brian is 8 years old. Ben is 2 years older than Brian. Blair is 2 years older than Ben.

1. How old is Brian?

8 yrs. old

2. How old is Ben?

10 yrs. old

3. How old is Blair?

12 yrs. old

4. How much older is Blair than Ben?

2 yrs. older

5. How much older is Ben than Brian?

2 yrs. older

6. Who is the oldest boy?

Blair

7. Who is the youngest boy?

Brian

8. How many years are the boys all together?

30 yrs.

©1996 Kelley Wingate Publications   71   KW 1301

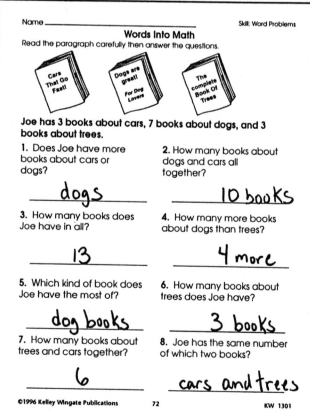

Name _____ Skill: Word Problems
Words Into Math
Read the paragraph carefully then answer the questions.

Joe has 3 books about cars, 7 books about dogs, and 3 books about trees.

1. Does Joe have more books about cars or dogs?

dogs

2. How many books about dogs and cars all together?

10 books

3. How many books does Joe have in all?

13

4. How many more books about dogs than trees?

4 more

5. Which kind of book does Joe have the most of?

dog books

6. How many books about trees does Joe have?

3 books

7. How many books about trees and cars together?

6

8. Joe has the same number of which two books?

cars and trees

©1996 Kelley Wingate Publications   72   KW 1301

Answer Key

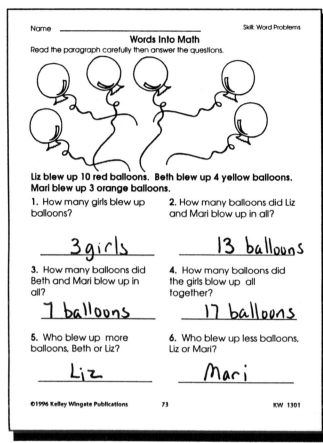

Name _____
Skill: Word Problems

Words Into Math
Read the paragraph carefully then answer the questions.

Liz blew up 10 red balloons. Beth blew up 4 yellow balloons. Mari blew up 3 orange balloons.

1. How many girls blew up balloons?

3 girls

2. How many balloons did Liz and Mari blow up in all?

13 balloons

3. How many balloons did Beth and Mari blow up in all?

7 balloons

4. How many balloons did the girls blow up all together?

17 balloons

5. Who blew up more balloons, Beth or Liz?

Liz

6. Who blew up less balloons, Liz or Mari?

Mari

©1996 Kelley Wingate Publications   73   KW 1301

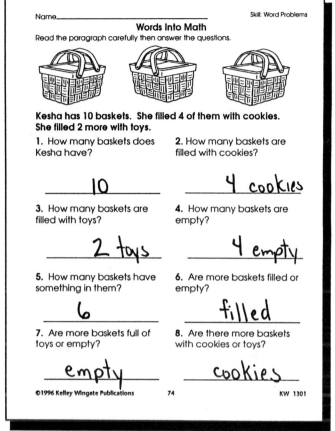

Name _____
Skill: Word Problems

Words Into Math
Read the paragraph carefully then answer the questions.

Kesha has 10 baskets. She filled 4 of them with cookies. She filled 2 more with toys.

1. How many baskets does Kesha have?

_10_

2. How many baskets are filled with cookies?

4 cookies

3. How many baskets are filled with toys?

2 toys

4. How many baskets are empty?

4 empty

5. How many baskets have something in them?

_6_

6. Are more baskets filled or empty?

filled

7. Are more baskets full of toys or empty?

empty

8. Are there more baskets with cookies or toys?

cookies

©1996 Kelley Wingate Publications   74   KW 1301

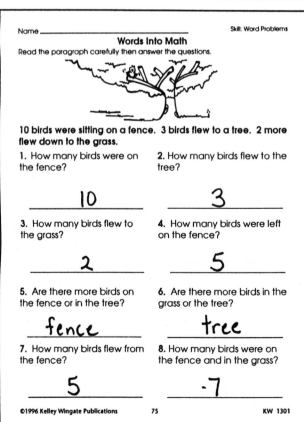

Name _____
Skill: Word Problems

Words Into Math
Read the paragraph carefully then answer the questions.

10 birds were sitting on a fence. 3 birds flew to a tree. 2 more flew down to the grass.

1. How many birds were on the fence?

_10_

2. How many birds flew to the tree?

_3_

3. How many birds flew to the grass?

_2_

4. How many birds were left on the fence?

_5_

5. Are there more birds on the fence or in the tree?

fence

6. Are there more birds in the grass or the tree?

tree

7. How many birds flew from the fence?

_5_

8. How many birds were on the fence and in the grass?

_7_

©1996 Kelley Wingate Publications   75   KW 1301

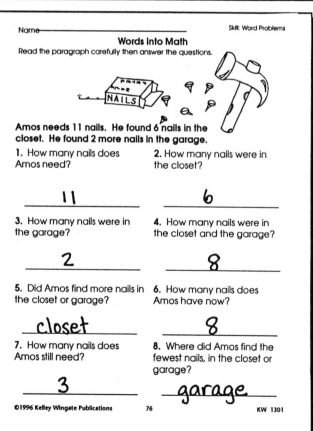

Name _____
Skill: Word Problems

Words Into Math
Read the paragraph carefully then answer the questions.

Amos needs 11 nails. He found 6 nails in the closet. He found 2 more nails in the garage.

1. How many nails does Amos need?

_11_

2. How many nails were in the closet?

_6_

3. How many nails were in the garage?

_2_

4. How many nails were in the closet and the garage?

_8_

5. Did Amos find more nails in the closet or garage?

closet

6. How many nails does Amos have now?

_8_

7. How many nails does Amos still need?

_3_

8. Where did Amos find the fewest nails, in the closet or garage?

garage

©1996 Kelley Wingate Publications   76   KW 1301

©1996 Kelley Wingate Publications   119   CD-3721

Answer Key

Words Into Math
Read the paragraph carefully then answer the questions.

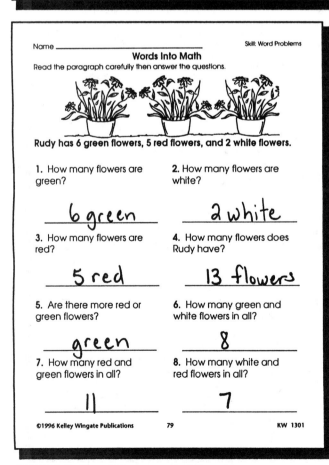

George has some dogs. He has 4 gray ones, 3 black ones, and 2 spotted ones.

1. How many dogs does George have in all?

9 dogs

2. How many dogs are gray?

4 gray

3. How many dogs are spotted?

2 spotted

4. Are there more black or spotted dogs?

black

5. How many gray and spotted dogs toether?

_6_

6. How many black and gray dogs are there?

_7_

7. Are there more black or gray dogs?

gray

8. How many black and spotted dogs are there?

_5_

©1996 Kelley Wingate Publications   77   KW 1301

Name _____ Skill: Word Problems
Words Into Math
Read the paragraph carefully then answer the questions.

Welcome To Our Class!

There are 12 children in the first grade class. 8 of the children are boys. 2 are seven years old. The rest are 6 years old.

1. How many children are in the class?

12 children

2. How many boys are in the class?

8 boys

3. How many girls are in the class?

4 girls

4. Are more children boys or girls?

boys

5. Are more children six or seven years old?

six

6. How many children are seven years old?

_2_

7. How many children are six years old?

_10_

8. Are there less boys or girls?

girls

©1996 Kelley Wingate Publications   78   KW 1301

Name _____ Skill: Word Problems
Words Into Math
Read the paragraph carefully then answer the questions.

Rudy has 6 green flowers, 5 red flowers, and 2 white flowers.

1. How many flowers are green?

6 green

2. How many flowers are white?

2 white

3. How many flowers are red?

5 red

4. How many flowers does Rudy have?

13 flowers

5. Are there more red or green flowers?

green

6. How many green and white flowers in all?

_8_

7. How many red and green flowers in all?

_11_

8. How many white and red flowers in all?

_7_

©1996 Kelley Wingate Publications   79   KW 1301

Name _____ Skill: Patterns
What Is Next?
Find the pattern in each series below. Draw the next three members of the series on the lines.

1. A B A B A B A B   __A__ __B__ __A__
2. A B C A B C A B   __C__ __A__ __B__
3. Z Z Y Z Z Y Z Z Y   __Z__ __Z__ __Y__
4. A A B B A A B B B   __A__ __A__ __B__
5. Z O P Z O P Z O   __P__ __Z__ __O__
6. A A A B B B A A   __A__ __B__ __B__
7. S G S G S G S G   __S__ __G__ __S__
8. W W T W W T W   __W__ __T__ __W__
9. A B A C A B A C   __A__ __B__ __A__
10. L M M L M M L M   __M__ __L__ __M__

Bonus: Design your own pattern of letters for your class to solve.

©1996 Kelley Wingate Publications   80   KW 1301

Answer Key

Worksheet 1 (page 81)

Skill: Patterns

What Is Next?

Find the pattern in each series below. Draw the next three members of the series on the lines.

1. # + # + # + # + __#__ __+__ __#__

2. = = + = = + = = __+__ __=__ __=__

3. (W W (W W (W __W__ __(__ __W__

4. P = # P = # P = __#__ __P__ __=__

5. + ○ # = + ○ # = __+__ __○__ __#__

6. F T F F T F T F F __T__ __F__ __T__

7.) # +) # +) # __+__ __)__ __#__

8. H I J H I J H I J __H__ __I__ __J__

Bonus: Design your own pattern for your class to solve.

81 KW 1301

Worksheet 2 (page 82)

Skill: Patterns

What Is Next?

Find the pattern in each series below. Draw the next three members of the series on the lines.

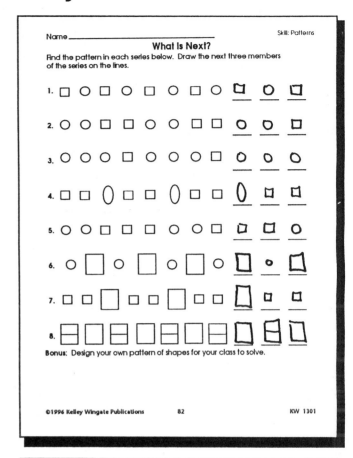

Bonus: Design your own pattern of shapes for your class to solve.

82 KW 1301

Worksheet 3 (page 83)

Skill: Patterns

What Is Next?

Find the pattern in each series below. Draw the next three members of the series on the lines.

1. (( )) # # ((__)__ __)__ __#__

2. (%) % (%) % __(__ __%__ __)__

3. O O O ⊘ O O O ⊘ __O__ __O__ __O__

4. ✔ X X ✔ X ✔ X X __✔__ __X__ __✔__

5. (squares pattern) __□__ __▨__ __□__

6. (divided circles pattern) __⊘__ __⊘__ __⊘__

7. ★ ★ ★ ☆ ★ ★ ★ ☆ __★__ __★__ __★__

8. ✦ ✦ ✦ ✱ ✱ ✦ ✦ ✦ ✱ __✱__ __✦__ __✦__

Bonus: Design your own pattern for your class to solve.

83 KW 1301

Worksheet 4 (page 84)

Skill: Patterns

What Is Next?

Find the pattern in each series below. Draw the next three members of the series on the lines.

1. 1, 2, 1, 2, 1, __2__ __1__ __2__

2. 10, 20, 10, 20, 10, __20__ __10__ __20__

3. 1, 2, 3, 1, 2, 3, __1__ __2__ __3__

4. 3, 4, 5, 3, 4, 5, __3__ __4__ __5__

5. 1, 10, 10, 1, 10, __10__ __1__ __10__

6. 1, 2, 3, 4, 5, __6__ __7__ __8__

7. 2, 4, 6, 8, 10, __12__ __14__ __16__

8. 1, 11, 2, 12, 3, __13__ __4__ __14__

Bonus: Design your own pattern of numerals for your class to solve.

84 KW 1301

Answer Key

Name_____
Skill: Patterns
What Is Next?
Find the pattern in each series below. Draw the next three members of the series on the lines.

1. 1, 10, 2, 20, 3, **30 4 40**

2. 1, 11, 2, 22, 3, **33 4 44**

3. 1, 2, 10, 20, 1, 2, **10 20 1**

4. 10, 9, 8, 7, 6, 5, **4 3 2**

5. 1, 2, 3, 1, 2, 3, **1 2 3**

6. 11, 22, 11, 22, 11, **22 11 22**

7. 3, 2, 1, 3, 2, 1, **3 2 1**

8. 4, 5, 44, 55, 4, 5, **44 55 4**

Bonus: Design your own pattern of numerals for your class to solve.

85 KW 1301

Name_____
Skill: Patterns
What Is Next?
Find the pattern in each series below. Draw the next three members of the series on the lines.

1. 1, 1, 2, 1, 1, 2, **1 1 2**

2. 8, 7, 6, 5, 4, **3 2 1**

3. 80, 70, 60, 50, 40, **30 20 10**

4. 800, 700, 600, 500, 400, **300 200 100**

5. 1, 2, 3, 4, 5, **6 7 8**

6. 10, 20, 30, 40, 50, **60 70 80**

7. 100, 200, 300, 400, 500, **600 700 800**

8. 1, 2, 1, 3, 1, 4, **1 5 1**

Bonus: Design your own pattern of numerals for your class to solve.

86 KW 1301

Name_____
Skill: Patterns
What Is Next?
Find the pattern in each series below. Draw the next three members of the series on the lines.

1. 11, 22, 33, 44, **55 66 77**

2. 1, 2, 1, 2, 1, **2 1 2**

3. 10, 20, 10, 20, 10, **20 10 20**

4. 1, 1, 2, 2, 3, 3, **4 4 5**

5. 1, 3, 5, 7, 9, 11, **13 15 17**

6. 5, 10, 15, 20, 25, **30 35 40**

7. 2, 4, 6, 8, 10, **12 14 16**

8. 1, 11, 2, 12, 3, 13, 4, **14 5 15**

Bonus: Design your own pattern of numerals for your class to solve.

87 KW 1301

Name_____
Skill: Telling Time
What Time Is It ?
Look at the clock below and answer the questions.

1. What time does this clock show?

_2:00_

2. It is daylight outside. Is this time A.M or P.M.?

_P.M._

3. What time will it be in one hour?

_3:00_

4. What time was it one hour ago?

_1:00_

5. Brad will eat dinner in three hours. What time will Brad eat dinner?

_5:00_

6. The baby just woke up. He slept for two hours. What time did he go to sleep?

_12:00_

88 KW 1301

Answer Key

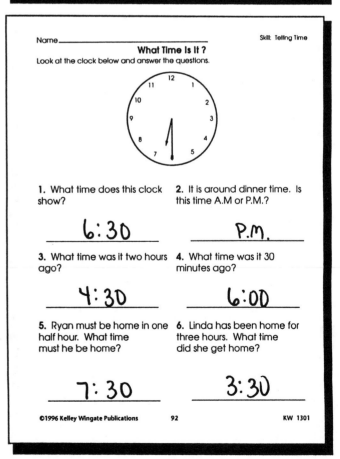

123 CD-3721

Top left worksheet (page 89):

Name_____   Skill: Telling Time
What Time Is It ?
Look at the clock below and answer the questions.

1. What time does this clock show?

9:00

2. It is daylight outside. Is this time A.M or P.M.?

A.M.

3. What time will it be in one hour?

10:00

4. What time was 2 hours ago?

7:00

5. Kyle eats lunch in three hours. What time does he eat lunch?

12:00

6. William woke up three hours ago. What time did William wake up?

6:00

©1996 Kelley Wingate Publications   89   KW 1301

Top right worksheet (page 90):

Name_____   Skill: Telling Time
What Time Is It ?
Look at the clock below and answer the questions.

1. What time does this clock show?

7:00

2. I just ate dinner. Is this time A.M or P.M.?

P.M.

3. What time will it be in four hours?

11:00

4. What time was it two hours ago?

5:00

5. Henry's bedtime is in two hours. What time does he go to bed?

9:00

6. Rachel ate dinner one hour ago. What time did she eat dinner?

6:00

©1996 Kelley Wingate Publications   90   KW 1301

Bottom left worksheet (page 91):

Name_____   Skill: Telling Time
What Time Is It ?
Look at the clock below and answer the questions.

1. What time does this clock show?

10:30

2. It is daylight outside. Is this time A.M or P.M.?

A.M.

3. What time will it be in one hour?

11:30

4. What time was it one hour ago?

9:30

5. Maria must read for half an hour. What time can she stop reading?

11:00

6. Erna will eat in two hours. What time will she eat?

12:30

©1996 Kelley Wingate Publications   91   KW 1301

Bottom right worksheet (page 92):

Name_____   Skill: Telling Time
What Time Is It ?
Look at the clock below and answer the questions.

1. What time does this clock show?

6:30

2. It is around dinner time. Is this time A.M or P.M.?

P.M.

3. What time was it two hours ago?

4:30

4. What time was it 30 minutes ago?

6:00

5. Ryan must be home in one half hour. What time must he be home?

7:30

6. Linda has been home for three hours. What time did she get home?

3:30

©1996 Kelley Wingate Publications   92   KW 1301

Answer Key

Skills Evaluation (page 93)

Skills Evaluation

Skill: Review

Choose the best answer to these review questions.
Circle the correct answer.

1. Add: 4
  +2
A. 24   B. 42
C. 6   D. 7

2. Subtract: 5
  - 3
A. 2   B. 3
C. 7   D. 8

3. Add: 9
  +3
A. 12   B. 13
C. 14   D. 49

4. Subtract: 12
  - 8
A. 20   B. 5
C. 4   D. 3

5. Subtract: 60
  - 20
A. 40   B. 50
C. 70   D. 80

6. Add: 75
  + 23
A. 52   B. 58
C. 92   **D. 98**

7. Subtract: 50
  - 10
A. 40   B. 20
C. 30   D. 60

8. Add: 40
  + 55
A. 95   B. 89
C. 97   D. 98

9. Subtract: 80
  - 30
A. 10   **B. 50**
C. 80   D. 60

10. Add: 45
  + 43
A. 82   **B. 88**
C. 62   D. 78

©1996 Kelley Wingate Publications   93   KW 1301

Skills Evaluation (page 94)

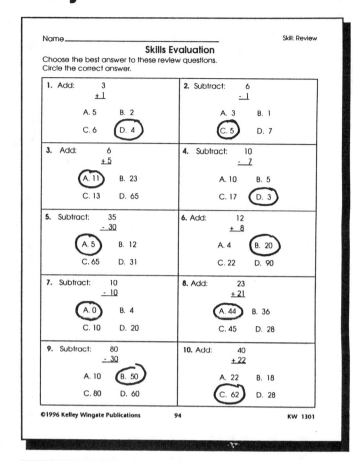

Skills Evaluation

Skill: Review

Choose the best answer to these review questions.
Circle the correct answer.

1. Add: 3
  +1
A. 5   B. 2
C. 6   **D. 4**

2. Subtract: 6
  - 1
A. 3   B. 1
C. 5   D. 7

3. Add: 6
  +5
A. 11   B. 23
C. 13   D. 65

4. Subtract: 10
  - 7
A. 10   B. 5
C. 17   **D. 3**

5. Subtract: 35
  - 30
A. 5   B. 12
C. 65   D. 31

6. Add: 12
  + 8
A. 4   **B. 20**
C. 22   D. 90

7. Subtract: 10
  - 10
A. 0   B. 4
C. 10   D. 20

8. Add: 23
  + 21
A. 44   B. 36
C. 45   D. 28

9. Subtract: 80
  - 30
A. 10   **B. 50**
C. 80   D. 60

10. Add: 40
  + 22
A. 22   B. 18
C. 62   D. 28

©1996 Kelley Wingate Publications   94   KW 1301

Skills Evaluation (page 95)

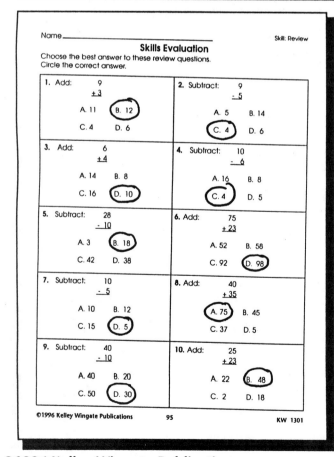

Skills Evaluation

Skill: Review

Choose the best answer to these review questions.
Circle the correct answer.

1. Add: 9
  +3
A. 11   **B. 12**
C. 4   D. 6

2. Subtract: 9
  - 5
A. 5   B. 14
C. 4   D. 6

3. Add: 6
  +4
A. 14   B. 8
C. 16   **D. 10**

4. Subtract: 10
  - 6
A. 16   B. 8
C. 4   D. 5

5. Subtract: 28
  - 10
A. 3   **B. 18**
C. 42   D. 38

6. Add: 75
  + 23
A. 52   B. 58
C. 92   **D. 98**

7. Subtract: 10
  - 5
A. 10   B. 12
C. 15   **D. 5**

8. Add: 40
  + 35
A. 75   B. 45
C. 37   D. 5

9. Subtract: 40
  - 10
A. 40   B. 20
C. 50   **D. 30**

10. Add: 25
  + 23
A. 22   **B. 48**
C. 2   D. 18

©1996 Kelley Wingate Publications   95   KW 1301

Skills Evaluation (page 96)

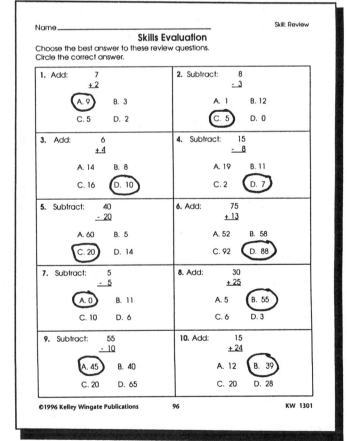

Skills Evaluation

Skill: Review

Choose the best answer to these review questions.
Circle the correct answer.

1. Add: 7
  +2
A. 9   B. 3
C. 5   D. 2

2. Subtract: 8
  - 3
A. 1   B. 12
C. 5   D. 0

3. Add: 6
  +4
A. 14   B. 8
C. 16   **D. 10**

4. Subtract: 15
  - 8
A. 19   B. 11
C. 2   **D. 7**

5. Subtract: 40
  - 20
A. 60   B. 5
C. 20   D. 14

6. Add: 75
  + 13
A. 52   B. 58
C. 92   **D. 88**

7. Subtract: 5
  - 5
A. 0   B. 11
C. 10   D. 6

8. Add: 30
  + 25
A. 5   **B. 55**
C. 6   D. 3

9. Subtract: 55
  - 10
A. 45   B. 40
C. 20   D. 65

10. Add: 15
  + 24
A. 12   **B. 39**
C. 20   D. 28

©1996 Kelley Wingate Publications   96   KW 1301

Answer Key

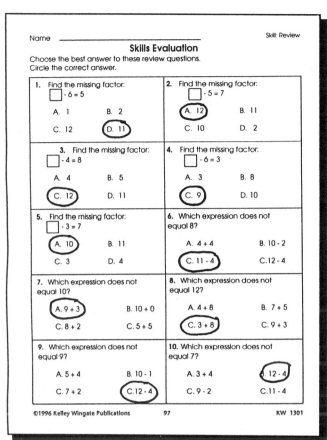

Name _____ Skill: Review

Skills Evaluation
Choose the best answer to these review questions.
Circle the correct answer.

1. Find the missing factor:
☐ - 6 = 5
A. 1   B. 2
C. 12   **D. 11**

2. Find the missing factor:
☐ - 5 = 7
A. 12   B. 11
C. 10   D. 2

3. Find the missing factor:
☐ - 4 = 8
A. 4   B. 5
C. 12   D. 11

4. Find the missing factor:
☐ - 6 = 3
A. 3   B. 8
C. 9   D. 10

5. Find the missing factor:
☐ - 3 = 7
A. 10   B. 11
C. 3   D. 4

6. Which expression does not equal 8?
A. 4 + 4   B. 10 - 2
C. 11 - 4   C. 12 - 4

7. Which expression does not equal 10?
A. 9 + 3   B. 10 + 0
C. 8 + 2   C. 5 + 5

8. Which expression does not equal 12?
A. 4 + 8   B. 7 + 5
C. 3 + 8   C. 9 + 3

9. Which expression does not equal 9?
A. 5 + 4   B. 10 - 1
C. 7 + 2   **C. 12 - 4**

10. Which expression does not equal 7?
A. 3 + 4   **B. 12 - 4**
C. 9 - 2   C. 11 - 4

©1996 Kelley Wingate Publications   97   KW 1301

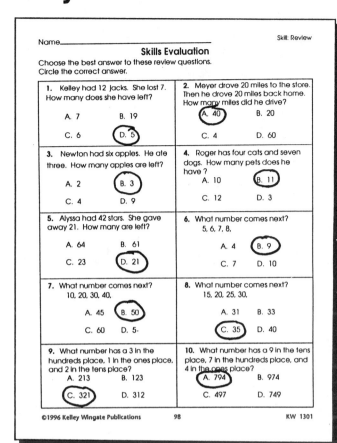

Name _____ Skill: Review

Skills Evaluation
Choose the best answer to these review questions.
Circle the correct answer.

1. Kelley had 12 jacks. She lost 7. How many does she have left?
A. 7   B. 19
C. 6   **D. 5**

2. Meyer drove 20 miles to the store. Then he drove 20 miles back home. How many miles did he drive?
A. 40   B. 20
C. 4   D. 60

3. Newton had six apples. He ate three. How many apples are left?
A. 2   **B. 3**
C. 4   D. 9

4. Roger has four cats and seven dogs. How many pets does he have?
A. 10   **B. 11**
C. 12   D. 3

5. Alyssa had 42 stars. She gave away 21. How many are left?
A. 64   B. 61
C. 23   **D. 21**

6. What number comes next?
5, 6, 7, 8,
A. 4   **B. 9**
C. 7   D. 10

7. What number comes next?
10, 20, 30, 40,
A. 45   **B. 50**
C. 60   D. 5.

8. What number comes next?
15, 20, 25, 30,
A. 31   B. 33
C. 35   D. 40

9. What number has a 3 in the hundreds place, 1 in the ones place, and 2 in the tens place?
A. 213   B. 123
C. 321   D. 312

10. What number has a 9 in the tens place, 7 in the hundreds place, and 4 in the ones place?
A. 794   B. 974
C. 497   D. 749

©1996 Kelley Wingate Publications   98   KW 1301

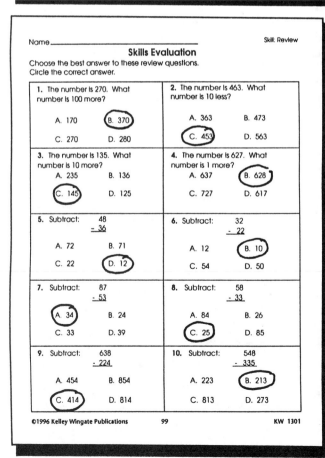

Name _____ Skill: Review

Skills Evaluation
Choose the best answer to these review questions.
Circle the correct answer.

1. The number is 270. What number is 100 more?
A. 170   **B. 370**
C. 270   D. 280

2. The number is 463. What number is 10 less?
A. 363   B. 473
C. 453   D. 563

3. The number is 135. What number is 10 more?
A. 235   B. 136
C. 145   D. 125

4. The number is 627. What number is 1 more?
A. 637   **B. 628**
C. 727   D. 617

5. Subtract:
48
- 36
A. 72   B. 71
C. 22   **D. 12**

6. Subtract:
32
- 22
A. 12   **B. 10**
C. 54   D. 50

7. Subtract:
87
- 53
A. 34   B. 24
C. 33   D. 39

8. Subtract:
58
- 33
A. 84   B. 26
C. 25   D. 85

9. Subtract:
638
- 224
A. 454   B. 854
C. 414   D. 814

10. Subtract:
548
- 335
A. 223   **B. 213**
C. 813   D. 273

©1996 Kelley Wingate Publications   99   KW 1301

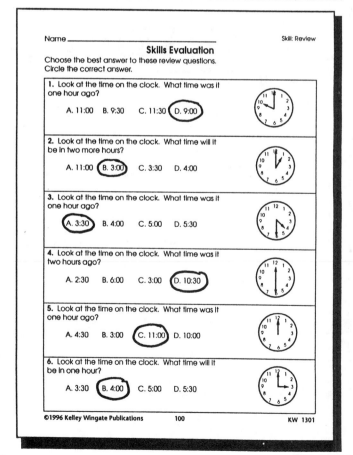

Name _____ Skill: Review

Skills Evaluation
Choose the best answer to these review questions.
Circle the correct answer.

1. Look at the time on the clock. What time was it one hour ago?
A. 11:00   B. 9:30   C. 11:30   **D. 9:00**

2. Look at the time on the clock. What time will it be in two more hours?
A. 11:00   **B. 3:00**   C. 3:30   D. 4:00

3. Look at the time on the clock. What time was it one hour ago?
A. 3:30   B. 4:00   C. 5:00   D. 5:30

4. Look at the time on the clock. What time was it two hours ago?
A. 2:30   B. 6:00   C. 3:00   **D. 10:30**

5. Look at the time on the clock. What time was it one hour ago?
A. 4:30   B. 3:00   **C. 11:00**   D. 10:00

6. Look at the time on the clock. What time will it be in one hour?
A. 3:30   **B. 4:00**   C. 5:00   D. 5:30

©1996 Kelley Wingate Publications   100   KW 1301

Addition Award

_____

receives this award for

_____

Keep up the great work!

_____ _____

signed   date

Amazing Addition!

_____

receives this award for

_____

Great Job!

_____ _____

signed   date

3 - 1	3 - 2	3 - 3	4 - 1
4 - 2	4 - 3	4 - 4	5 - 1
5 - 2	5 - 3	5 - 4	5 - 5
6 - 1	6 - 2	6 - 3	6 - 4

3   0   1   2

4   0   1   2

0   1   2   3

2   3   4   5

5 + 7	5 + 8	5 + 9	6 + 6
6 + 7	6 + 8	6 + 9	7 + 7
7 + 8	7 + 9	8 + 8	8 + 9
9 + 9	1 - 1	2 - 1	2 - 2

12 14 13 12

14 15 14 13

17 16 16 15

0 1 0 18

$\begin{array}{r} 2 \\ +\ 9 \\ \hline \end{array}$	$\begin{array}{r} 3 \\ +\ 3 \\ \hline \end{array}$	$\begin{array}{r} 3 \\ +\ 4 \\ \hline \end{array}$	$\begin{array}{r} 3 \\ +\ 5 \\ \hline \end{array}$
$\begin{array}{r} 3 \\ +\ 6 \\ \hline \end{array}$	$\begin{array}{r} 3 \\ +\ 7 \\ \hline \end{array}$	$\begin{array}{r} 3 \\ +\ 8 \\ \hline \end{array}$	$\begin{array}{r} 3 \\ +\ 9 \\ \hline \end{array}$
$\begin{array}{r} 4 \\ +\ 4 \\ \hline \end{array}$	$\begin{array}{r} 4 \\ +\ 5 \\ \hline \end{array}$	$\begin{array}{r} 4 \\ +\ 6 \\ \hline \end{array}$	$\begin{array}{r} 4 \\ +\ 7 \\ \hline \end{array}$
$\begin{array}{r} 4 \\ +\ 8 \\ \hline \end{array}$	$\begin{array}{r} 4 \\ +\ 9 \\ \hline \end{array}$	$\begin{array}{r} 5 \\ +\ 5 \\ \hline \end{array}$	$\begin{array}{r} 5 \\ +\ 6 \\ \hline \end{array}$

8	7	6	11
12	11	10	9
11	10	9	8
11	10	13	12

1 + 1	1 + 2	1 + 3	1 + 4
1 + 5	1 + 6	1 + 7	1 + 8
1 + 9	2 + 2	2 + 3	2 + 4
2 + 5	2 + 6	2 + 7	2 + 8

5	4	3	2
9	8	7	6
6	5	4	10
10	9	8	7

8 − 8	9 − 1	9 − 2	9 − 3
9 − 4	9 − 5	9 − 6	9 − 7
9 − 8	9 − 9	0 − 0	−
+	>	<	=

6 7 8 0

2 3 4 5

minus 0 0 1

equals   less than   greater than   plus

6 - 5	6 - 6	7 - 1	7 - 2
7 - 3	7 - 4	7 - 5	7 - 6
7 - 7	8 - 1	8 - 2	8 - 3
8 - 4	8 - 5	8 - 6	8 - 7

5 6 0 1

1 2 3 4

5 6 7 0

1 2 3 4